UNIX SYSTEM
SECURITY ESSENTIALS

compliments of

Tiffany A. Moore
PUBLICITY COORDINATOR
CORPORATE & PROFESSIONAL PUBLISHING GROUP

Addison-Wesley Publishing Company
ONE JACOB WAY
READING, MASSACHUSETTS 01867
(617) 944-3700 EXT. 2714 FAX: (617) 944-7273
INTERNET: tiffanym@aw.com

UNIX SYSTEM
SECURITY ESSENTIALS

Christoph Braun

Siemens Nixdorf

ADDISON-WESLEY
PUBLISHING
COMPANY

Wokingham, England • Reading, Massachusetts • Menlo Park, California • New York
Don Mills, Ontario • Amsterdam • Bonn • Sydney • Singapore
Tokyo • Madrid • San Juan • Milan • Paris • Mexico City • Seoul • Taipei

The programs in this book have been included for their instructional value. They have been tested with care but are not guaranteed for any particular purpose. The publisher does not offer any warranties or representations nor does it accept any liabilities with respect to the programs.

Many of the designations used by manufacturers and sellers to distinguish their products are claimed as trademarks. Addison-Wesley has made every attempt to supply trademark information about manufacturers and their products mentioned in this book. A list of the trademark designations and their owners appears below.

Cover designed by Designers & Partners of Oxford
and printed by The Riverside Printing Co. (Reading) Ltd.
Typeset by VAP Group Ltd., Oxford
Printed and bound in Great Britain at Biddles of Guildford

First printed 1994.

ISBN 0–201–42775–3

British Library Cataloguing-in-Publication Data
A catalogue record for this book is available from the British Library.

Library of Congress Cataloging-in-Publication Data applied for.

Trademark Notice
SINIX™ and WX200™ are trademarks of Siemens Nixdorf Informationssysteme AG
X Window System™ and Kerberos™ are trademarks of Massachusetts Institute of Technology
OSF/Motif™ and Distributed Computing Environment™ (DCE) are trademarks of Open Software Foundation Inc.
UNIX™ is a trademark of AT&T

Contents

5   Planning security management   77

6   Important commands and system calls   93

Chapter 1
Introduction

This book is concerned with how a variety of UNIX operating system users can keep the system secure. The manual is intended for all users of UNIX systems and for those who have to make decisions about such systems, without using them themselves.

This manual is not an introduction to the UNIX operating system. It assumes the reader already has a basic knowledge of the operating system. The reference system for this manual was SINIX V5.41, installed on a WX 200 from Siemens Nixdorf Informationssysteme AG. SINIX is the Siemens Nixdorf implementation of UNIX System V Release 4. If not stated otherwise, all discussions in this book relate to System V, but much of the detail will be relevant to users of other systems, too.

Many people have contributed to this book. I thank Peter Collinson, Petra Froehlich, Ingo Hoffmannn, Rita Nisius, and Ursel Ritterhoff, who all read drafts and made valuable comments. Claus Noack and Michael Rust from Siemens Nixdorf Informationssysteme AG supplied the managerial support to write this book. Special thanks go to Nicky Jaeger, Susan Keany and Susanne Spitzer, who provided valuable editing.

Guide to the manual

Chapter 2 describes the mechanisms for UNIX system security for users who do not have system administrator privileges. You should read Chapter 2 when you begin to work with UNIX.

Chapter 3 explains the system administrator's tasks necessary to establish and monitor a secure system.

Chapter 4 is directed at the developers of system and application programs on UNIX systems. It describes the measures necessary to integrate a program into the security concept of a UNIX system.

Chapter 5 is a general description of the problems of system security. In addition, it provides suggestions for the development and realization of a thorough security concept.

Chapter 6 provides short descriptions of commands and system calls that have relevance for system security for system administrators, programmers, and non-privileged users.

Conventions

The following conventions are used in this handbook:

⚠	for cautionary notes
italic	for commands, variables, constants and options in text
`Courier`	for terminal output in examples
`Courier`	for command input in examples
`$`	input prompt for non-privileged users
`#`	input prompt for system administrators

Chapter 2
Security for users

User mistakes and negligence are the most common causes of threats to data security. This chapter is concerned with the critical threats to data security that UNIX systems users should recognize, avoid and overcome.

2.1 The UNIX operating system

If you use a computer to solve some problem, you will run an application program, for example, a word processor program. But to be able to run, that program needs a set of other programs, comprising the so-called 'operating system' of your computer. UNIX is such an operating system.

2.2 What UNIX security means to users

As a user of the UNIX operating system, you need a basic understanding of what you can do to protect information within your computer and access to the resources of the computer, and how security affects users.

Security for a computing system means that the system is protected as much as possible against manipulation, user errors, natural disasters and technical malfunction. There are three main areas of protection: integrity of data, privacy of information, and availability of computer resources.

3

Availability means that all users can access the resources and functions of the system for its correct operation. Loss of this availability is called 'denial of service'.

Integrity of data files and programs means preservation of their contents against all unauthorized change. An object that has lost its integrity is said to be corrupted. The concept of integrity also applies to the computer as a whole. For the system to retain its integrity, it has to retain the value of its components.

For certain objects, integrity alone is not sufficient to ensure their value. They must not be accessible to unauthorized persons and their privacy must be protected. For example, the value of files containing marketing data would diminish if their contents were known to a competitor.

The UNIX computer operating system provides an interface between you, the user of the computer, and the computer. You can access the computer via the operating system, using commands, library routines, functions and programs that allow you to tell the computer how to process and store the information that belongs to you.

A computer system takes care of security by deciding who is authorized to access which information. To to be able to do that, UNIX has to identify each user on the system uniquely and store information in files, each of which belongs to a single user. UNIX System V performs these tasks through the use of the login and passwd (password) mechanisms, which identify you to the system; also included in the UNIX security mechanisms are access mode bits, so that users can make access decisions, that is, decide which other users can access their files.

Security has its price, of course. As a rule of thumb, we might say that you have to pay for increased security with less user friendliness in a computer system. But the gain of your (and your customers') confidence in the integrity and privacy of data stored in your computer is more than worth that price. UNIX makes it quite easy to pay it.

2.3 Connection with UNIX

The first action taken by a user of a UNIX system is to establish a connection with the computer on which UNIX is installed and to log in to the system. UNIX has mechanisms that prevent access by users who have no login privileges. The effectiveness of the UNIX security mechanisms depends critically on their correct use by those who do have access privileges.

2.3.1 User login names

In order for you to gain access to the UNIX system, you must log in. As an authorized user, you know your user name and password, which you must type in before you can work in your login account. For example, if your login name is *michael*, your login line will look like this:

```
login: michael
```

Next, the system will ask you for your password. Your screen will look similar to this:

```
login: michael
password:
```

If you try to log in with a user name not in the system (that is, not in the file */etc/passwd*), the system will still ask for a password before it denies access, returning the message:

```
Login incorrect
```

You will get another `login` prompt and a second chance to log in.The UNIX system behaves similarly, supplying the same message, if a known user name is given but is followed by an incorrect password. When trying various user names and passwords, potential intruders cannot find out what they did incorrectly after a failed login attempt: whether both user name and password were wrong, or a correct user name was given but an incorrect password, or a correct password was given but not the user name to which it belongs.

Normally, it is not very difficult to guess user login names. UNIX user names are usually the first or last names of the users. For example, the user login name of the user Hal Falkenberg could be

- `hal`
- `falke`
- `hf`

or something similar. If no information is available, a list of common first and last names might provide enough information to guess a user login. Once users have access to a system, whether authorized or illegal, they can find out the login names of other users. The commands *who*, *find* or *finger* will provide some logins, or one can simply look at the file */etc/passwd* which contains all user names. Obviously, system access is not protected by user login names, which is why secure passwords are crucial to system security.

2.3.2 Choosing passwords

In theory, the most secure passwords consist of random combinations of letters, both upper and lower case, numbers, punctuation marks and special characters. Such a password is, of course, nearly impossible to remember. If you don't want to burden your memory with it, you can write it down, which immediately creates another problem, namely, keeping it hidden. Someone who wants to know your password need only watch you as you log in: you will reveal the place where the password is kept – in a desk drawer, in your address book, on a note stuck under your keyboard or desk, or in some other place.

Thus the password must be kept in your head and nowhere else. One way to accomplish this is to use abbreviations of words or sentences. If possible, you can utilize numbers as in, for example, '1derful' or 'be4login'. You can take a sentence that is easy to remember and abbreviate the words, for example: 'to be or not to be' becomes '2bon2b'. You increase the security of your password when you make use of as many different types of characters as possible. Instead of a password solely made up of lower-case letters, mix in upper-case letters, punctuation marks and special characters.

Another way to create a more secure password is to select two short words separated by some arbitrary punctuation mark. There is a practically inexhaustible number of such word pairs and punctuation mark characters. If you take this password and substitute upper-case for one or two of the lower-case letters, the potential 'password cracker' has practically no chance.

Passwords can have up to eight characters. Longer passwords can be used but UNIX will evaluate only the first eight characters. So, UNIX will not distinguish a difference among the words 'confidence', 'confidential', and 'confidentiality', although each is unique, because the first eight characters are identical.

Use a combination of the various character types available on your keyboard, but do not use characters or character combinations that serve to delete characters or whole lines. Use the command *stty* for showing delete characters.

Depending on your system, the terminal may interpret the character combination CTRL–H as an instruction to delete the last character typed in; CTRL–X may enable you to delete the current line you are typing. The functionality for character and line deletion can be assigned to other character strokes by changing the file *.profile*, but such changes only take effect after the login is complete. During the login procedure, while the user is typing in the user name and password, the standard assignments are in effect.

During login, the password is not displayed on the screen as it is being typed, which prevents others from reading it. You should also take care that no one can watch as you type the password. Otherwise, you might disclose all or part of your password when someone notices the keys you press.

2.3.3   Password encryption

UNIX encrypts passwords. This prevents users from knowing other users' passwords, even if they manage somehow to read the password file (usually */etc/passwd*). Each time you type in your password, it is compared to the result of a first password encryption stored in the password file of your system. If the result of the typed-in password encryption matches the stored result, you are granted system access.

UNIX uses an encryption algorithm based on the Data Encryption Standard (DES). For password encryption, DES has been modified in a way that makes it impossible to reverse the encryption. Once a password is encrypted, it cannot be known from the encryption result. There is no known way to decrypt passwords, if you have only the result of the encryption.

But you can crack passwords by guessing. A cracker selects likely passwords, encrypts the passwords, and looks for matches in the password file. Likely passwords are chosen from a dictionary enhanced with additional entries. These entries are generated following certain rules. Example rules for additional password guesses from the dictionary entries could be:

- Duplicate the word, so that anne becomes anneanne
- Reverse the word back-to-front
- Append character 'x' to the word
- Prepend character 'y' to the word
- Force the word to lower case
- Force the word to upper case
- Substitute 'x' for 'y' in the word

To prevent successful password cracking, you have to choose a password that is not contained in any dictionary and cannot be generated from a dictionary by following simple rules.

2.3.4   Shortcomings of passwords

To test your password, try to imagine that you are the unauthorized user who is trying to guess your password. Here are several options you could consider:

- You could try passwords that contain or refer to the name of the user, his or her initials, user login name or perhaps other personal information. For example, say you are trying to find out the password for a user named 'David H. Brenner', who has the login name *david*. Some guesses that might yield success could include: david, david0, david1, david123, dhb, dhbdhb, dbrenner, DBrenner, rennerb, divad, DhbbhD, BRENNER, (david).
- You could use a number of word lists. These might include lists of common proper names, geographic placenames, famous persons, titles, characters and scenes from films and science fiction, figures from mythology, legends, fairy tales and the Bible, and abbreviations, all of which can be gleaned from various relevant reference texts, as well as sports terminology, including team names and nicknames. You could try numbers, strings

of digits such as, for example, '4949', or written out like 'nineteen', especially birthdates such as '110862'. Include lists of strings of adjacent keys on the computer keyboard (for example 'qwerty', 'asdf', or 'zxcvbn'), machine names (listed in the file /etc/hosts) and finally the words of the complete English dictionary or another locally spoken language.

- Next, alter the words of your word lists. Capitalize the first letter of the word, insert a special character at the beginning of the word, reverse the order of the letters (with and without the capitalization), change the letter 'o' into the number '0' (changing something like 'word' into 'w0rd'), change the letter 'l' into the number '1', 'z' into '2' and 's' into 5. Alter the nouns so that they are plural.

- Experiment through combinations of upper- and lower-case letters that you haven't tried already, that is, an upper-case letter in the middle of the word (from 'david' do you get the password 'dAvid', 'daVid', or 'davId'?), two upper-case letters ('DAvid', 'DaVid', and so on are possibilities), three upper-case letters in the word, and so on. The number of possible combinations mixing upper and lower-case rises dramatically with the number of letters that differ from the original spelling of the word.

- Now try word pairs. The number of possibilities is overwhelming in this case, too. To keep this test to a manageable size, limit it to words from your word lists that are only three or four letters long. Even with that limitation, the number of possible word pairs will be in the millions.

As the above description of a break-in attempt shows, if a password can be found on any word lists, it can be guessed by a determined attacker. The spectacular 'successes' of intruders (also called 'hackers' or 'crackers') do not much depend on a thorough knowledge of the system they are attempting to invade. Two things make it possible to break into a computer: the authorized users' simple, and therefore insecure, passwords and the persistence of the intruder.

If the *uucp*-connection is unprotected or there are security loopholes in *sendmail*, *ftp*, or *tftp*, an unauthorized user will be able to look through the /etc/passwd file, which can be read by all users and contains all login names. Should an intruder manage to get system administrator permissions, he or she could read the file /etc/shadow and, using a personal computer, decipher the passwords. This can be accomplished by taking the words of a word list, like the one described above, that includes all possible names and variations with mixed upper and lower-case, and encrypting each one. Then, the encrypted word from the word list is compared to the encrypted password from /etc/shadow. For passwords derived from English words, the dictionary file /usr/dict/words can be used as a starting point.

The history of spectacular computer break-ins has shown that the overwhelming majority of users utilized 'secure' passwords, which effectively hindered the intruder. However, there were a few users who had extremely insecure passwords, passwords found on a simple word list. The intruder can achieve the best success rate by simply trying as the password the account name or the name of the person whose account they are attempting to break into.

2.3.5   Changing passwords

To improve the effectiveness of your password's security, you should change your password regularly, for example every month or two. Using 'password ageing', some systems force users to change their passwords periodically. If your system administrator assigned you this type of ageing password and the password has expired, you will not be allowed to log in to the system until you have chosen a new password. Your screen will look something like this:

```
login: michael
Password:
Your password has expired.
Choose a new one.
Old password:
New password:
Re-enter new password:
$
```

The system is informing you that your ageing password is no longer valid, and it requires you to choose a new one. Then it prompts you for your old password; you should type in your expired password. After that, you are requested to type in a new password, which must differ from the old password by at least three characters. When you have typed in your new password, the system will prompt you to type it in again, in order to double check it. If you make a mistake the second time you type it in, the system will notify you and return to the first prompt requesting your new password. When the two new passwords match, you will be given access to the system; the system responds with the input prompt.

   If your system administrator has given you a temporary password, it is possible that you will not be able to change your password for a certain amount of time, determined by the administrator. Otherwise, it is possible to change your password at any time. When you do this with the command *passwd*, your screen will look like:

```
$ passwd
Changing local password for michael on alibaba
Old password:
New password:
Re-enter new password:
$
```

Before you are allowed to change your password, you must enter your current password. The purpose of this is to be sure that only you can change your password, not anyone who might have access to your terminal when you have left it without logging out. If you make a mistake typing in your old password, the system will reply with the error message Sorry. The password will remain unchanged and you will have to repeat the command *passwd*. If the old password is entered correctly, you will be prompted for the new password. Since the passwords don't appear on the screen, the system checks for accuracy by requiring you to enter the new password twice. In this way, it ensures that any typing mistakes will not be interpreted by the system as part of the correct password. If the password differs each time, the password remains unchanged:

```
$ passwd
Changing local password for michael on alibaba
Old password:
New password:
Re-enter new password:
They don't match; try again
$
```

When choosing a new password, it is important that you choose one that is truly new. Often, users find it easy just to switch back and forth between two passwords. If an unauthorized user finds out one of the two, he or she need only wait until you change back to that password.

Choose different passwords for the various systems where you have logins. That way, if an intruder has figured out your password on one system, you prevent him or her having the potential to immediately access all the other systems.

A good secure password is important even if you think your user account does not contain any sensitive information. As an authorized user, you play a part in the responsibility for the entire system's security: a potential attacker could use your poorly secured user account as an open door for invasion of the whole system. This is also true on a network. If an intruder discovers your password on a less secure machine, he or she could use the opening to get access to other, more secure machines that contain more sensitive data.

2.3.6   Anomalies of login

If you get unfamiliar messages while logging in, you should ask your system administrator whether the messages are correct. You should be particularly suspicious when your password seems to fail and you get the message:

```
Login incorrect
```

In this case, it could, of course, be caused by a simple typing mistake; however, it could also be that a fake login program is running, also referred to as a 'spoofing program'. It generates an apparently normal greeting on the screen of a particular terminal and waits for a user to log in to the system. The program reads the user name and password as the unsuspecting user types them in, and sends them to the originator of the spoofing program.

As soon as the user has given away his or her login name and password in this way, the spoofing program prints the message

```
Login incorrect
```

The unsuspecting user now thinks that he or she typed in the password incorrectly. The spoofing program exits, giving control back to the real login program. The user can then log in without even suspecting the deception.

If you suspect that a spoofing program is trying to spy on you to get your user name and password, log out using the key combination CTRL–D and turn off your terminal. Do not finish logging in. Tell your system administrator about the unusual behaviour of the system. Log in to the machine at a secure terminal and change your password, with *passwd*, immediately.

Enhanced UNIX versions (meeting special security requirements) prevent spoofing programs from working by using what is called a **trusted path** which means that there is a secured transmission path between the computer and the terminals. The user of a trusted path does not get the login prompt until a certain key combination is pressed (called the Secure Attention Key, or SAK). When the SAK is pressed, a trusted path is established between that terminal and the machine. The trusted path exists only during the normal login procedure and is then replaced with a normal data transmission path.

2.3.7 Telephone connections

When you want to connect to the UNIX machine via a modem and telephone line, use the command *cu.* Then you enter the telephone number. As soon as the terminal prints the message

```
ONLINE
```

the connection has been established successfully. The message BUSY means that the telephone line is busy and that you should try dialling the UNIX machine again; NO ANSWER means that a connection is impossible. If this happens, you should check for problems with the connections between terminal, modem and telephone lines. Once you have established the connection to UNIX successfully, press the key XX and you will then get the login prompt. From this point on, the login procedure will function as it does on a terminal directly connected to the system.

A telephone connection is a security issue since any user can dial into your UNIX system. Therefore, you need to be certain that unauthorized users do not have access to your telephone and modem. Make sure that the telephone number of the machine remains secret, and that when you log out, your modem actually hangs up, cutting off the telephone connection. Otherwise, an unauthorized user could gain access to your user account.

When you hang up, terminating the telephone connection, you should automatically be logged off the system. However, you should not depend on this. Always log off the system explicitly before you terminate the telephone connection to the system.

The *cu* command does not make any integrity check on data it transfers. Data with special *cu* characters may not be transmitted properly. After making the connection, *cu* runs as two processes: the transmit process reads data from the standard input and passes it to the remote system; the receive process accepts data from the remote system and passes it to the standard output. With the *cu* command *~%put*, you initiate a transmit process, and with the *cu* command *~%take* you start a receive process.

2.3.8   Access with chipcards

UNIX controls system access using the knowledge of the user: if the user knows the password that corresponds to the login account, permission to access the account is granted. Products that rely strictly on the user's distinguishing features or on the possession of some object offer more secure access control. This means, for example, products that rely on fingerprints, the pattern of the hand, the cornea of the eye, speech patterns, the way keys are pressed, or simply the possession of a chipcard.

Chipcard systems consist of hardware components (chipcards, chipcard readers, encrypting devices) and security software, which are installed on the UNIX system to which access is being controlled. The user identifies himself to the machine by inserting his chipcard into the chipcard reader and then entering a secret number known only to the chipcard owner.

2.3.9   Security of terminals

When you have logged in to the system, a prompt for input appears on your terminal. The terminal is like a door to the UNIX system that can be opened with the 'keys', the user name and password. As you log out, you are effectively closing the door and locking it. An unauthorized user can gain access to your account only by using the 'skeleton key', that is, a password that has been discovered.

When you leave your terminal without logging out, any other user can access your user account. Your terminal becomes like an open door, through which anyone can enter. For this reason, you should log out every time you leave your terminal, even if it will just be for a short time. In that short interlude, an intruder can cause tremendous damage for which you could be responsible.

If it seems cumbersome to you to restart your work where you left off, after you have logged out and logged in again, you can write a UNIX procedure or a program that will block your terminal instead. To cancel the block, you must enter a password. It is more secure, however, to log out entirely every time you leave the terminal. Some blocking programs can be killed with a break signal from the keyboard. A spoofing program could be set up to spy on your password. If you use a blocking program, you must be cautious that the program is designed to ensure security.

2.3.10   Intelligent terminals

Intelligent terminals, including personal computers, can occasionally be programmed so that, via a keystroke or a signal from the main machine, the current data on the screen could be obtained. Many terminals can send a line from the screen back to the machine when a control character sequence or escape sequence is entered. This is as if the line had been entered directly at the keyboard. An intruder could abuse this 'answer back' terminal capability to send data to your terminal using the *write* command for example, thus initiating undesirable actions. An example could be data sent to the terminal that contained the message

```
rm -rf $HOME <send current line to the system>
```

When this line appears on the screen, it will be sent to the system to be executed as a command at the next prompt. If you are using an intelligent terminal, you should stop other users from sending messages to your terminal. You can do this with the command

```
mesg -n
```

It is recommended to add this to your file *.profile*.

For the duration of your login session, this will block other users from sending messages, such as with the *write* command. However, it will not block messages from the system administrator sent with *wall* or *write*. These messages are always sent to the terminal.

Occasionally, programs on personal computers behave as if the PC were a UNIX system terminal. When this is the case, there is a program running on the PC that imitates, that is, emulates, the functionality of a UNIX terminal. Terminal emulations often store interactions on the PC disk, so that they can send the stored interactions to the system in place of the user's actual terminal input.

Fake terminal emulations can be used like spoofing programs, trying to find out the user's password. The problem can only be solved by going back to your original emulation program, which has been stored securely. This should be reinstalled if you ever become suspicious that a malevolent user or intruder has installed a fake terminal emulation on your PC.

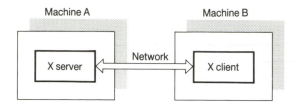

Figure 2.1   X client and X server on a network.

2.3.11   Graphics terminals and the X Window System

The X Window System gives other users read and write access to your output display. The X Window System is based on the client–server concept, that is, an X window application program, the 'X client', does not directly administer input and output. The X client gives the tasks of administering input and output devices (screen, keyboard, and mouse) to an independent process, the X server. The X server transforms X client output requests into actual screen output and forwards the user's input to the X client.

X clients and servers communicate in order to transmit user input and output tasks to each other. Interprocess communication is used for communication between a client and a server running on the same machine. If the X client and server are running on two separate machines, the processes communicate over the network (Figure 2.1).

The default setting for most X window implementations is to turn external host access off. But generally speaking the X server is available for all X clients. This means that all X clients can access the server's resources – the display, keyboard input, windows or mouse input. It does not matter where the X client is running. If your machine is on a public network such as Internet, your display is essentially accessible from X clients on other machines worldwide. This normally desirable feature can easily be abused by malicious users if they can get access to the X server.

Another user could use the Xlib function *XQueryTree*( ) to determine the ID of one of your windows and its children. This is the only information needed for malicious users to be able to write in your windows. For example, they can use the program *meltdown*, which makes the display image 'melt'. It is even possible for them to call the X window library function *KillClient*( ) to destroy another user's X server.

If a 'spy' has access to the X server, he or she will be able to observe the contents of the other user's window using *xwd* or *xwud*, programs that are widely available. In addition, using the X window functions *XGetImage*( ) and *XPutImage*( ), an unauthorized user can copy the contents of another user's window to his or her own screen.

These and other possible manipulations depend on an X server that is openly accessible to all X clients.

Machine-specific access control

Using the X client *xhost*, you can update the internal access list of the X server. This access list determines which machines an X client can be running on to be allowed to access the X server. You can use the X client *xhost* both for local displays and for X terminals.

In the case of **local displays**, the list of machines to be allowed access is initialized when the X server is started, using the configuration file */etc/Xn.hosts*, where *n* indicates the number of the display to which access will be controlled. Usually, only one display is associated with a workstation, so that the configuration file is called */etc/X0.hosts*. Entries for X terminals that will be allowed access to the X server are also in the file */etc/X0.hosts*.

For example, the file */etc/X0.hosts* on the host machine *galilei* could include the following entries, that indicate which machines may have access to the X server:

```
leonardo.mit.edu
einstein.eu.net
planck.quant.de
galilei.ans.com
```

Only the system administrator is allowed to make changes to the entries for local displays and X terminals. As a non-privileged user, you can use *xhost* to add machines (*xhost* +machine), remove access permission (*xhost* – machine), eliminate all access restrictions (*xhost* +) or eliminate all access permissions (*xhost* –). You can only start *xhost* from a machine on which your X server is located. If you try to invoke *xhost* from a remote machine, you will get the error message:

```
xhost: must be on local machine to add or remove hosts
```

The *xhost* mechanism should only be used to add access capability for a remote machine when you can be certain that all users of the machine are trustworthy.

User-specific access control

Beginning with X11R4, another mechanism is available for allowing targeted individual users access to a display. To enable this mechanism, allowing **user-specific** assignment of access permissions, the following entries under *local* displays must be in the *xdm* configuration file */usr/lib/X11/xdm/xdm-config*:

```
DisplayManager._0.authorize: true
DisplayManager*authorize: false
```

The first entry enables the user-specific access control for the local display. You use the second entry to tell *xdm* that it should work for other displays without user-specific access control.

When the local X server is started with *xdm*, it receives a session key, also called the 'Magic Cookie' from *xdm* in a file in the directory */usr/lib/X11/xdm*. At the start, *xdm* gives the file name to the X server. Thereafter, the local X server only allows access to the X clients that can give the session key.

If a user successfully logged in to the *xdm* opening screen, *xdm* stores the session key in the file *$HOME/.Xauthority*. All X clients the user starts for the display get the session key from the file *$HOME/.Xauthority* and pass it to the X server. The X server will deny access to other users' X clients, because these foreign X clients cannot give the current session key. When this happens, the display shows the error message

```
Client is not authorized to connect to Server
```

The X server of an **X terminal** cannot be started by *xdm*; instead, the server is automatically loaded when the X terminal is turned on. Thus, *xdm* sends the session key for the X server over the XDMCP net protocol to the X terminal. The X server permits access only to the X clients can pass the correct session key.

If a user successfully logs in to the *xdm* opening screen of the X terminal, *xdm* stores the session key in the *$HOME/.Xauthority*. All X clients the user starts for the display get the session key from the file *$HOME/.Xauthority* and pass it to the X server.

When an X session is ended and another is started, a new key is generated and given to the X server. The file *$HOME/.Xauthority* has the access permissions $--rw-------$, which allow read and write access only to the owner. To ensure that user-specific access protection actually works, you should not change the access permissions of the file *$HOME/.Xauthority*. Furthermore, no other users should have read or write capabilities for your home directory. Otherwise, another user could read or alter the file in spite of the restricted access permissions on the file *$HOME/.Xauthority*: the access restrictions on this file are only as secure as your home directory.

In the case of X terminals, the setting of *true* or *false* in the *xdm* configuration file does not alone determine whether user-specific access control is enabled or disabled. If the X server of an X terminal requests that it be used, *xdm* will enable user-specific access control for the X terminal, regardless of the configuration file entry.

If you have enabled user-specific access control with the entry in */usr/lib/X11/xdm/xdm-config*, the *xdm* opening screen could display the message

```
This is an unsecure session
```

This warning message means that the X server of this X terminal does not support user-specific access control or that the user-specific access control is not activated on this X terminal. However, if user-specific access control is disabled in the *xdm* configuration file, no warning message will be displayed.

You have to set some X terminals specifically, so that the X server uses user-specific access control. To find out whether the X server of an X terminal can utilize user-specific access control, refer to the X terminal documentation.

Say you want to output something from your login on a remote machine to your display. Before you can do this, you must get the key from the file *$HOME/.Xauthority* on the remote machine and enter it into the file *$HOME/.Xauthority* in your home directory. The X client *xauth* does this extraction and entry:

```
xauth [ f key_file] [-vqib] [command arguments]
```

Usually *xauth* is used to extract the key for the current display, transfer it to a remote machine, and enter it in the same user's key file on the remote machine:

```
$ xauth extract - $DISPLAY | rsh remote_machine xauth merge -
```

For example, you can use the key for the display *leonardo:0* for your user login on the remote machine *galilei*:

```
$ xauth extract - leonardo:0 | rsh galilei xauth merge -
```

If the authorization mechanism functions properly, the X client *xhost* should display the following message:

```
access control enabled (only the following hosts are allowed)
```

If a list of machines that are allowed access accompanies this message, for each machine you will need to explicitly deny X server access:

```
xhost - <machine_list>
```

This is the only way to prevent users gaining access from remote machines, entered via *xhost* in the list of machines allowed access. When you are using user-specific access control, *xhost* should return an empty list.

If you are working with the X Window System on X terminals, you can lock your display screen without needing to obtain or write a UNIX script or program beforehand. The X Window System includes the user application (the X client) *xlock*, which you can use to lock access to the display administration or 'X server.' The lock is removed when the user enters the correct login password.

2.3.12   Logging out from UNIX

When you have finished your session on the UNIX system, log off. On most terminals, you do this by pressing CTRL–D (hold down the CTRL key and simultaneously press 'd'). This input does not appear on the screen, since it is an unprintable character. The UNIX system replies with the login prompt, which is waiting for some user to login:

```
$ CTRL-D
login:
```

You have logged out successfully and have started a new login. In place of CTRL–D, you can also use the command *exit*.

When you are logging out, it is most certainly not sufficient just to switch off your terminal or, if you are logged in over a telephone line, simply to hang up the telephone. If you do this, it is possible that your login connection will remain open and anyone could use the system as if they were you. Some terminals actively prevent a logout if the terminal is turned off. Therefore, it is imperative that you actually log yourself out with CTRL–D or *exit*, or *logout*, respectively, every time you leave your terminal.

2.4   Files and directories

Your system's data is stored in files. Every file belongs to a directory. If you want to protect your data so that confidentiality, integrity and accessibility are maintained, you must protect the files and directories of your system.

2.4.1   Files and access permissions

The access permissions of a file establish which users are allowed to perform which actions on the file. The access permissions allow three different types of actions:

- read access to the file
- ability to write to the file
- execution of the file (when the file is a program or shell procedure)

Users belong to three categories:

- owner of the file, who determines the accessibility for all normal users
- user group
- all others

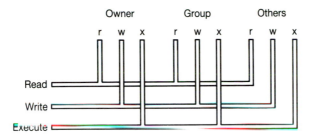

Figure 2.2 Permissions.

You can ascertain the access permissions of a file by using the command *ls –l*:

```
$ ls -l README
-rwxr--r-- 1 michael   project   12301   Jun 21
10:00 README
$
```

The permissions are shown in the leftmost column. Within that column are three subcolumns, from left to right, for 'owner', 'group', and 'others'. In each column of a user classification are the actions allowed for that set of users: **r** stands for permission to read the file, **w** to write to the file, and **x** to execute the program or other UNIX procedure. If you looked at a file where all three classifications of users have permission to perform all three types of actions, *ls –l* would output the letters in the order shown in Figure 2.2.

There can be a minus sign '–' in any of the positions corresponding to the actions **r**, **w**, or **x** and corresponding to the category of users. This means that action is not allowed for that classification of user. In many commands and system calls, these permissions are expressed as octal numbers:

```
1 = execute
2 = write
4 = read
```

A combination of access permissions is expressed by the result of adding the component permissions. If you combine read and write permissions, you will use the result of 2 + 4 = 6. So, the number '6' symbolizes the rights to read from and write to a file. For the combined read, write and execute permissions, you will get the number '7' (from 1 + 2 + 4). An octal number for each of the three categories of users (owner, group, others) shows the combination of permissions for that user class. All the access rights for a file are expressed with a three-digit combination of numbers. For example, the number '777' means that the owner, group, and others all have read, write and execute rights. Table 2.1 shows some samples of combinations of access rights.

Table 2.1   Examples of combinations of access permissions.

Symbolic representation	Octal representation	Meaning
– – – – – – – – –	000	No access to any user
r – – – – – – – –	400	Only the owner is allowed read access
r w – r – – – – –	640	The owner has read and write permission, the group has read access
r w x r w x r w x	777	All types of access rights for owner, group, and others

You, as 'owner', can determine the protection level of your files. Users of enhanced UNIX systems meeting B2 *Orange Book* security have even more exact control over which specific users can access a file. Using what are called access control lists (ACLs), the user can define exactly which individual users are allowed access to the data objects. The system administrator can classify the level of confidentiality of files and other data objects using mandatory access control or MAC, setting which users receive what access authority.

Access permissions allow you to perform the following actions:

- Read access means that you may read or copy a file. Shell procedures need only read permission to be executable.

- Write access means that you can change or abbreviate the file. If you have only write permission you will not be able to edit the file. However, you can copy a readable file to it, so that the contents of the write-only file will be overwritten by the contents of the readable file. Of course, if you copy an empty file to the write-only file, the contents of the write-only file will be deleted.

- Execute permission allows you to run a file that is a program or shell procedure. Shell procedures must be both readable and executable in order for the system to be able to read the commands in the procedure. For programs, only the execute permission is required.

- The I-bit has the effect that a program, by using the C library function *lockf()*, can lock the file for as long as the program has access to the file.

2.4.2   Setting permissions

The owner of a file can change or set the permissions of that file by using the command *chmod*, which requires a string argument that gives the permissions followed by the file names. The permissions can be given in the three-digit octal representation or in symbolic form:

```
[who]changes[which perms][,[who]changes[which
perms]]..
```

You use *who* to indicate for which user category you want to change permissions:

u   (**u**ser) for the owner
g   (**g**roup) for the group
o   (**o**thers) for others
a   (**a**ll) for all users

In *changes*, you state whether you want to add, delete or reset permissions:

+   add access permission
−   take away access permission
=   reset access permissions, overwriting previous permissions

You use *which perms* to declare which permissions you want to add or delete. The argument *which perms* can be a combination of the following options:

r   read
w   write
x   execute
l   lock (for mandatory locking)

Say you have an executable file *program*, and you also have read and write permissions for it. In order to prevent yourself from accidentally changing your file, you can use *chmod* to remove your own write privileges. After you have run the command, look at the new permissions with *ls −l*:

```
$ chmod u-w program
$ ls -l
total 35
-r-xr-xr-x    1 michael    project    9346 Nov 1
08:32 program
$
```

To assign the permissions shown in the previous example, you could also use the octal number representation:

```
$ chmod 555 program
```

The command *umask*, which sets the maximum permissions for all files and directories that are created after its invocation, functions in the opposite manner. The command sets which access permissions new files will not receive. Thus, the command *umask 007* says that the owner and group will be allowed all types of access (0 = no permissions are taken away), while others are not allowed any permissions (7 = all permissions are refused). If you want to know the current *umask* setting for your user account, call *umask* without arguments:

```
$ umask
077
$
```

An invocation of *umask* doesn't have any effect on the capability to change permissions with *chmod*. When you are determining access permissions, allow only as many permissions as is absolutely necessary for that class of users ('need-to-know principle'). You need to apply this principle to yourself, as well. Thus, at the very least, you should by default disallow the write privilege for 'others' (*umask 002*). In this case, you and all the members of your group can read and write to the file. With *umask 022*, you prevent the group from having write permission. The best defence against others' access for newly created files is *umask 077*. Then, only you, the owner, have read and write access to the files. The files will become accessible to the other users only when you explicitly set the appropriate permissions with *chmod*.

2.4.3   Access permissions for directories

Directories are actually nothing but files themselves. The data in a directory file consists of information about the files and other directories contained in it. Directories have access permissions for owner, group, and others just as other files do. They differ from regular files in that the directory provides a table of the files it contains as well as their corresponding permissions. The permissions of the directory itself apply to the directory, not to its member objects.

     In the listing of information about files and directories in the current directory, you can distinguish a directory by the *d* in the first column:

```
$ ls -l
drwx- - - 2 michael   project  837 Dec 5 16:58
security
drwx- - - 1 michael   other    539 May 8 09:43
manuals
$
```

If you have read permission for a directory, you can use the command *ls* to get information about the directory. If you do not have execute permission for the directory, you will not be allowed to use *ls -l* to get more detailed information. The combination of write and execute permissions allows you to add files to or delete files from the directory. If you have execute permission, you are allowed to search through the directory, which means that you can make it your current directory or use it as part of a path.

   To create, add, or delete a file, you need write and execute permissions for the directory that contains or will contain the file. The permissions on the files themselves are unimportant:

```
$ ls -ld  memos memos/memo1
drwxrwxrwx 1 michael project 164 Aug 27 15:09 memos
-r---- 1 michael project 907 Aug 30 09:52 memo1
$ rm -r memos/memo1
rm: memos/memo1: 400 mode? y
$ mkdir memos
$ cp /home/tom/trick memos/memo1
$ chmod 400 memos/memo1
$ chown -R michael memos
$ ls -l memos/memo1
-r---- 1 michael project 1023 Sep 5 17:03 memos/memo1
$
```

In this example, the file *memo1* in the directory *memos* was replaced with */home/tom/trick*, although no user had write permission on the file. Even when a file has no permissions at all, someone could delete and add files. The only requirement is for the user to have write and execute privileges on the directory. The warning

```
   memos/memo1: 400 mode?
```

notifies you that you don't have appropriate permissions on the file, but this can be ignored with the answer 'y'. Thus, the access protection of a file is only as good as the protection provided by the directory. Consequently, you should be just as careful assigning permissions to directories as you are to files. Using *umask 077* you can ensure that newly created directories will not have read, write, or execute rights for anyone but you. If you want to better protect your files by restricting access to your already existing directories, use *chmod*:

```
   $ cd
   $ find . -type d -exec chmod 700 {} \;
   $
```

If you just want to give execute permission to others, substitute *chmod 711* for *chmod 700*.

2.4.4   The startup file .profile

When you log in you have the capability to set defaults needed for your work on the system or to execute commands. You can have this done automatically by entering the settings and commands in the file *.profile* in your login directory. Your entries there become effective when you log in to the system. The file *.profile* is also executed if you are working with the OSF/Motif-based user interface, because all terminal emulations start a login shell which uses *.profile* as the start file. Using a resource entry in the configuration file *$HOME/.Xdefaults*, you can ensure that the terminal emulations you start use a login shell and therefore execute the file *.profile*:

```
Client for Terminal-Emulation*LoginShell: True
```

If you change your *.profile* and want the changes to take effect in the current session, execute it as a shell procedure:

```
$ cd
$ . .profile
$
```

The first entry in *.profile* should be the search path. Every time you start to run a program, your shell will look for it in system directories given in the search path. The shell variable *PATH* is assigned the list of directories that should be searched for programs and commands. The command *echo $PATH* will give you the value of your current search path:

```
$ echo $PATH
:/usr/bin:/usr/sbin:/home/michael/bin
$
```

In this example, the search path contains the three directories */usr/bin*, */usr/sbin*, and */home/michael/bin*. The directories are separated by colons.

The search path can lead to security problems. If one of the directories in the search path is not properly protected, a malicious user could replace some program in the directory with a Trojan horse program. This is a program that has been changed so that it appears to successfully produce the expected results, but at the same time, starts unwanted side-effects built into it by the intruder. You call some program, for instance, and an executable program by that name is found in your search path. You could be executing a Trojan horse program that has the same name as the program you called.

A secure search path begins with the directories that contain most of the commands, */usr/bin* and */usr/sbin*. Other directories can be included, perhaps your current directory. In your search path variable *PATH* the current directory is represented by a colon at the beginning or end of the path, a double colon or a period. Better security can be maintained if you do not include the current directory in your search path. This is because you could change your directories and your current directory might then be an unprotected directory, which could contain a Trojan horse. If absolutely necessary, you could put your current directory as the last directory in your search path.

A search path should not contain directories in which every user has write permission. For example, the directory /tmp should never be a member of a search path.

If you want to call a program in your current directory, you can add the characters ./ to the beginning. If, for example, you want to run your 'private' *ls* program which is in the current directory, execute it with *./ls*. This way you can be sure that you are running your own program.

Directories belonging to other users should not be in your search path. If you want to use other users' programs, make your own copy in your private program directory. If you use the program very seldomly, you can also simply use its absolute path name.

It is always risky to use unknown programs. Programs belonging to other users are out of your control. Use such a program only when you can be sure that it does not contain a Trojan horse.

As well as setting your search path in *.profile*, you should set the default access permissions for new files with *umask*. The most secure setting is

```
umask 077
```

Enter this in your *.profile*.

You should also stop other users using the command *write* to send messages to your terminal that could be interpreted as commands, thereby threatening the security of your system. Some terminals interpret certain control characters so that the current line of the screen is sent to the machine. The line written to the screen is then interpreted as input from the terminal. In this way, a message line sent from *write* can contain an unpleasant surprise for the recipient, for example if it is the following:

```
rm -rf $HOME <send the current line to the
machine>
```

When the victim receives the message with this line, it will be sent to the machine and executed as a command: all files in the recipient's home directory will be deleted. To prevent such an attack, enter the following command in *.profile*:

```
mesg n
```

If you use the C shell, you can use the startup file *.cshrc* to improve the security of your system. You may use the same commands as in *.profile*.

Table 2.2   User id is normally inherited by a child process of a user's login shell.

Process	/bin/sh	/bin/du
Real user	michael	michael
Real group	project	project
Effective user	michael	michael
Effective group	project	project

Under some versions of the C shell, it is possible to set the autologout variable to log you out after a specified number of minutes of idle time. For example, if you specify in your *.cshrc*:

```
set autologout=15
```

you will be logged out automatically after you have been idle for 15 minutes.

2.4.5   Programs with the s-bit

Along with the access privileges for read, write, and execute on files, there is another type that only applies to programs: the 's-bit' for owner and group. If an s-bit is set, the process created when the program is executed will run with the same effective user or group number as the owner or group of the file, rather than that of the user who is running the program.

Each user has two sets of ids for *user* and *group*. One set is called the **real user id**, the other set contains the **effective user id**. The latter may be changed by the s-bit for user and group, respectively.

Normally, the real and the effective user ids are inherited from the login shell. They remain the same during the course of a login session. When a new process is invoked, a child process of the login shell is created, which has the same set of ids as the user's login shell. For example, if you use **du** to summarize disk usage, the user id sets will look like Table 2.2.

When you invoke a program with the s-bit, the newly created process inherits the user id of the owner of the invoked program, instead of inheriting the effective user id of the parent process. This is necessary for programs which have to be shared by many users, such as the *mail* or *passwd* commands.

For example, when a user invokes the write command, which copies lines from your terminal to that of another user, the user is granted write access to the terminal of the other user. For security reasons, users are not normally allowed access to each other's terminals. For *write*, the s-bit for group is *tty* (Table 2.3).

The effective group id of the *write* process is not *project*, as would be the case under normal circumstances, but *tty*. Because every user's terminal is writable by the group *tty*, the s-bit for *group* of the command *write* permits the access that would normally be denied. Generally, the s-bit is set to grant access to

Table 2.3   The effective group id while using the write command is tty.

Process	/bin/sh	/bin/write
Real user	michael	michael
Real group	project	project
Effective user	michael	michael
Effective group	project	tty

files that are not accessible by 'normal' users, who do not have privileges. Another example of this principle is the *passwd* command. It gives users permission to write to the password file (*/etc/passwd* or */etc/shadow*), even though it is only writable by the superuser.

If the s-bit is set for the owner or group at the same time that the x-bit is set, for permission to execute, then there will be an *s* in place of the *x*:

```
$ ls -l /bin/passwd
-rwsr-sr-x 1 root   sys   23056 Apr 28 1994
/bin/passwd
```

Without the corresponding x-bit, the s-bit cannot be set.

The s-bit provides temporary exceptions to the normal access permissions, so that you can, for instance, change your password, get information about free disk space, use the commands *mail* and *uucp*, or look at the system's process table. This does not bear a security threat in itself, because a program can do only what it has been designed to do. But many people have discovered ways of making an s-bit program perform something that its originators did not intend it to do. Generally speaking, if there is an s-bit, there also is the possibility of misuse. If an s-bit gives you the privilege of *root*, the potential security risk cannot easily be underestimated. You can do almost anything in your system, as soon as you figure out a way of using the s-bit to run programs as the superuser.

2.4.6   Setting s-bit and and sticky bit permissions

You can recognize which programs have the s-bit set by looking at the listing output of *ls –l*. The s-bit is represented in the permissions by an *s* in the execute *x* position. You can see some examples of this by looking in */usr/bin*, which could look like this:

```
-r-sr-xr-x 1 root   sys    34388 Jul  4 1992 at
-r-x--s--x 2 bin    mail   94380 Jul  4 1992 mail
-r-xr-xr-x 1 bin    bin    10192 Jul  4 1992 mkdir
-r-sr-sr-x 1 bin    sys    23220 Jul  4 1992 passwd
```

Having the s-bit set on these programs does not create a security problem. This is because access to protected files is limited to the actions performed by the command program. The s-bit is only a problem if it makes it possible to access files that should not be accessible.

Normally, a user does not need to own s-bit programs. If you do have such programs in your directories, you should know why the s-bit is necessary. If you find it necessary to own an s-bit program, make sure its access permissions are set so that no other users can read or write to the program. Otherwise, remove the program or its s-bit, using *chmod*:

```
ls -lc /usr/bin/cracker
-r-sr-xr-x 1 root    other    220858 May  2 13:13
/usr/bin/cracker
# chmod u-s /usr/bin/cracker
# ls -lc /usr/bin/cracker
-r--r-xr-x 1 root    other    220858 Jul 30 7:08
/usr/bin/cracker
```

Instead of *chmod u–s*, you can use the numeric arguments to *chmod*. The number 4000 sets the user id bit, and 2000 sets the group id bit:

```
# chmod 4755 /usr/bin/cracker
# ls -lc /usr/bin/cracker
 -rwsr-xr-x 1 root     other   220858 Aug 15 11:23
/usr/bin/cracker
```

In the *x* position for 'others', there can also be a *t* or *T*, which indicate that a status bit called the sticky bit (t-bit) is set. *T* indicates that the sticky bit is set without the x-bit; *t* indicates a set sticky bit when the x-bit is set. Only the system administrator can set the sticky bit. If an unauthorized user attempts to set the sticky bit, it will be ignored. When the executable program is read in from the program file, this bit signals that the program does not have to be swapped out to the hard disk swap area.

Two flags in addition to those discussed in Section 2.4.2 are the set-user-ID and set-group-ID attributes, or s-bit for owner and group.

2.5   Commands and system programs

When you're working on the system, you and all other users will use commands and system programs that could relate to security problems. The following subsections explain some ways to avoid problems that could result from using such commands and programs.

2.5.1   cp

The command *cp* copies the contents of a file to another file. The permissions on the target file remain the same since only the contents are copied. However, if *cp* creates a new file, the new target file will get the access permissions of the original file. This rule is not true for programs that have the s-bit set. When you copy an s-bit program, thereby creating a new program file, the new file will no longer have the s-bit.

The *cp* command ignores the default *umask* settings. For this reason, copying could create objects that are not protected as intended with the *umask* settings. Check through your directories regularly for these, looking for the objects that do not have sufficient protection.

2.5.2   crypt

Using the command *crypt* you can encode and decode texts that you want kept confidential. *crypt* uses a simple encrypting technique, which is relatively easy for an unauthorized user to 'crack', for example using the widely available program 'Crypt Breaker's Workbench (*cbw*)'.

For this reason you should only use *crypt* when there is no other encryption program available. To increase the security of an encryption using *crypt*, take the following precautions:

- Compress the files before you encrypt them. Compression, using one of the commands *compress* or *pack*, transforms any straight text which the unauthorized user could read with a program like *cbw*. If an unauthorized decryption attempt does not find any normal text, *cbw* will not be able to determine whether it has been able to translate your encoded text correctly.

- To decode a compressed file, the unauthorized user could use the header added by the command *compress* which lists the files that were compressed. This header contains the hexadecimal values 1f, 9d and 90 (in this order). After you compress the file, strip off the header using the command *dd*:

```
$ dd if=secret.Z of=secret.Z.strip bs=3 skip=1
```

Then before you uncompress the file, add the header to the file again:

```
$ compress -cf /dev/null; crypt <encrypted
```

Encode your files several times with crypt, each time using a different key.

2.5.3   mv

The remarks about *cp* in the previous section also apply to *mv*. This command changes the name of the file, not the contents. You can use *mv* to change the name of an s-bit program without changing its permissions. Unlike *cp*, the *mv* command does not change the owner of the file, provided the old and new file (path) names are on the same file system.

If it is used to move files between different file systems, *mv* actually uses *cp*. The original file is copied, its owner is changed, and then the original is deleted. Thus, if some other user moves your s-bit program to another file system, that user will become the owner and you, the original owner, will no longer have access to the file.

2.5.4   ln

The command *ln* creates links, or references, to files. By using links, you can refer to the same file with various file names and paths.

Using *ln*, you can set up a link to another user's file. In the link file, *ln* maintains all attributes that apply to the original file – owner, group, and permissions remain the same in the new link file. The *umask* settings are ignored by *ln*.

Changes to file permissions are valid for all its links. That is, if you change the permissions of a file, all links to it will likewise change.

Use *rm* to remove the link that you created with *ln*. If there were more references to it, you will still be able to access the file using the remaining link(s). When you delete an s-bit program, you should check whether there are more links to it. This is the only way you can know for certain whether your program was really deleted. The file isn't deleted until all its links are also deleted. Before you delete a file, see how many links it has:

```
$ ls -l pascal
-rws--s--x   2 michael project 1734 Apr 1 16:15
pascal
$
```

The second column (after the permissions and before the name of the file's owner) shows the number of links. In the example, there are two links to the file *pascal*, one of which is the file itself. If you delete *pascal*, the file will still exist under the name of the remaining link.

This remaining link could possibly be in a directory for which you have no access rights; you would not be able to determine the file or path name. Even if you do know where the link is, it could be that the permissions on the other directory prevent read or write access.

Therefore, before you remove one of your own files, you should always ensure that all other links to the file are removed at the same time. Only then can you know that the file will no longer be accessible to any user. If you cannot ensure that all links have been deleted, strip away the access rights to the file:

```
$ chmod 000 pascal
$ rm pascal
$
```

This way, all access permissions have been removed from the file, so that the remaining link loses its capabilities for other users. Instead of deleting the file, you can also overwrite its contents:

```
$ > pascal
$ ls -l
-rws--s--x   2 michael project    0 Apr 1 16:15
pascal
$
```

Using output redirection to the file without any input will delete its contents. All links to *pascal* are now completely useless.

2.5.5   su

The command *su* enables you to work under another user login account without having to log off the system and log in again. Assume you are logged in to the system as the user *michael* but you want to work under the account *peter*. You can use *su* to change accounts, first identifying yourself as an authorized user with the password for the account:

```
$ su peter
Password:
$
```

The command *su* gives you all the access permissions of the user account *peter*. At the same time, you lose the permissions you had under the original account. The system administrator (the user name *root*) enters the *root* password to change to any user's account without having to enter any other password. For this reason the *root* password must be particularly protected from the curiosity of unauthorized users. When changing to an account with *su*, all the security rules and guidelines are the same as when you log in directly to the account.

2.5.6   newgrp

System V UNIX allows users only to reside in a single group. You can use *newgrp* to change to another user group, which means that you change your group permissions. When you create new files, their group permissions will take on those of the group to which you changed using *newgrp*. You can use *newgrp* to change to any group in which you are a member. If a password is associated with the group in the file */etc/group*, then *newgrp* will prompt you for it:

```
$ newgrp alpha
Password:
$
```

You can only log in to a group in which you are not a member if it has a password associated with it.

Under Berkeley UNIX, users can reside simultaneously in all groups in which they are included by an entry in */etc/group*. Therefore, Berkeley UNIX users don't need the command to change between groups.

2.5.7   The vi editor

If the editor *vi* or the system crashes, you can later recover the file you were editing at the time using the *vi* option *–r*. In order to make this recovery possible, *vi* stores a temporary file in the generally accessible directory */tmp*. Other users could easily tamper with this file or replace it with another file of the same name if the sticky bit is not set, in order to make the file only accessible to the owner.

You can avoid this problem using the variable *EXINIT*. *EXINIT* can be assigned the name of the directory which *vi* should use as the storage place for your temporary files. To prevent other users from being able to access your temporary files, assign *EXINIT* a private directory, one which only you can access. Put your *EXINIT* definition in *.profile* and export the variable.

The setting of *EXINIT* has precedence over any contradictory settings in *$HOME/.exrc*, which defines the user environment for *vi*.

2.6   Archiving data

Using disks and magnetic tape you can make backup copies of data, transport it, and read it into other systems. These activities can endanger the confidentiality of your data or, if you read in software that contains a Trojan horse, it could compromise the integrity of the system.

2.6.1   Data media

Data media containing confidential information are usually stored in a central archive; however, sometimes the disks and tapes are stored by an individual user. The best protection for data on storage media is a locked container like an office safe. Ordinary office cabinets and desk drawers are not suitable for storing confidential data.

Create a catalogue listing of your storage media and keep it separate from the media themselves. This makes it easy to check whether any items are missing. Don't mark the outside of the media with any information about their contents. Instead, use an archive number system, so that the archive number marked on storage media references a corresponding entry in the catalogue.

Follow the media manufacturer's guidelines for storage and shipping. Always keep records of the transfer and shipping of media to another department or firm. If you are planning to send out reused storage media, you should reformat the media first before writing to them. This ensures that the media hold only the data you intend to send.

If storage media become defective or are otherwise no longer necessary, their disposal should be controlled carefully. Before you destroy them, delete their contents by reformatting the media or by using a magnetizing instrument. This is the only way you can be certain that the data on the media is deleted.

2.6.2   Archiving and reading files

The commands *tar* and *cpio* can be used to write data to storage media or read data from them. Since practically every UNIX system has a unique set of user names, IDs, groups and file system structure, you should always use relative pathnames. Before you read data into the system, verify the contents of the data media:

```
$ cpio -itv </dev/fd0
```

If you use the *tar* command, enter:

```
$ tar tv /dev/fl2
```

Using these command options, you produce a table of contents of a disk. The device file */dev/fd0* stands for the disk drive of your computer. Under UNIX, the access to devices, such as magnetic tape and disk drives, is controlled just like the access to files. For one physical device there can be several different device files that accommodate different access methods. You may find an overview of device files in the UNIX documentation.

When reading data objects from external media, you should first read them into a temporary directory under your user account. This directory should not be accessible to anyone but you:

```
$ mkdir tmp
$ chmod 700 tmp
$ cpio -id </dev/fd0
```

The access permissions of the files read in will remain as they were originally on the media read in. However, the user and group of the files will be that of the user who read in the files. After you have read in the files and checked them, you can move or copy them to their final location.

2.7 Exchanging mail

Using the commands *mail* and *mailx*, mail messages can be sent and received. These commands put your message into a file that belongs to the recipient.

There is a potential security problem with using *mail* and *mailx*: the sender does not have to be the actual user who appears in the head of the message. If you get a message from another user on the same system, it is easy to obtain the real sender's name in the message's 'from' line. However, if the message comes from another system, it becomes difficult to establish who the actual sender is. If it is important to know who the sender is, then you should find an alternative to *mail* and *mailx* for exchanging information. For example, you could use a secure exchange of physical storage media.

Lines that begin with an exclamation mark ! are interpreted by mail as commands that are to be executed by the shell. If you send a mail message that begins with a string of characters that includes a colon, you must insert a blank line before the first line of the message.

2.8 Malicious programs

System security can be endangered not only by the user's negligence but also by programs that execute unauthorized or even criminal activities. To limit such programs as much as possible you should see to it that all programs you use come from trustworthy sources. A malicious program can have particularly devastating effects if it obtains superuser privileges and uses them to control all access permissions.

2.8.1 Viruses

A virus is a code fragment which, inserted in a program, executes along with the program making copies of itself in other programs. Viruses are not isolated programs and cannot run by themselves. In order for viruses to have an effect, they need programs to 'infect'. When a program including the virus is executed by a user, the virus will be activated. The virus code tries to find other executable programs that the user is allowed to modify, and copies itself there.

Viruses spread most commonly on personal computers, systems that have practically no security provisions. This makes virus propagation easier. So far, UNIX virus attacks have not been as widespread as they are on personal computers. But viruses have been written for UNIX systems, and the potential for trouble is there.

Most of the protection against UNIX viruses lies with the system administrator. But there are several things a non-privileged UNIX user can do to improve one's resistance to infected software:

- Careful use of access permissions to prevent unauthorized access to object, shell script and system initialization files. Make sure your directories are writable only by you. Set the *umask* to *077*. At the least, you must set the *umask* to *027* to remove group write permission on newly created files and to prevent *others* from reading, writing, or executing anything in the directory.

- Correct setting of the *PATH* and *IFS* shell variables to prevent corresponding file attacks. Put system directories first in your *PATH*. Don't include '.' in the *PATH*.

- Scanning of incoming code files for suspect code. Don't trust a program if you don't have to. Don't trust software from public sources. Don't run a program you don't trust. Any program has the potential of carrying a virus.

Once your system has been attacked by a virus, it is very difficult to recover. It can take several days to do so. It is better to prevent any virus attack in the first place.

To help with this task, you can use the COPS system, which makes a check of file system permissions. You can get COPS via anonymous *ftp* from *cert.seic-mu.edu*, in the directory *ftp/pub/cops*. If you cannot make contact with this site, you may contact Dan Farmer under *df@cert.sei.cmu.edu*. Dan Farmer and Eugene H. Spafford are authors of 'The COPS Security Checker System', a paper presented at the summer 1990 USENIX Conference in Anaheim. Public USENIX source archives (Volume 22 of *comp.sources.unix*) provide COPS, as well as many UNIX vendors and many major computing sites.

2.8.2   System files open to manipulation

The files especially vulnerable to manipulation are those that the system reads during the login process to set up the user's environment.These files should be checked often to ensure that their access permissions do not offer opportunities to other users. Also, check whether the settings of these initialization files ease manipulation by other users (for example, by setting *umask* to allow very 'generous' access to other users). Depending on which shell you are using, the initialization files are shown in Table 2.4.

Table 2.4   UNIX initialization files.

Shell	File	Function
sh ksh	.profile (in the user's login directory)	Settings and commands that are executed after login
sh ksh	/etc/profile	System-defined settings and commands that are executed after a user logs in
csh	.cshrc (in the user's login directory)	Settings and commands that are executed when a C-shell is started
csh	.login (in the user's login directory)	Settings and commands that are executed when a C-shell user logs in to the system
csh	.logout (in the user's login directory)	Settings and commands executed when the user logs out from the system
ksh	.kshrc (in the user's login directory)	Settings and commands that are executed when the user starts a Korn shell

2.8.3 Worms

Worms are program files that duplicate themselves, wandering from system to system using computer networks. The most famous example of a UNIX worm was the Internet worm of November, 1988 (named the Morris worm after its originator). To multiply itself, this worm typically took advantage of operating system loopholes (in the Berkeley 4.3 version of UNIX). Other worms spread by taking advantage of deficiencies in networking software.

All worms must break the password security which is supposed to protect against unauthorized intrusion into the system. The Internet worm overcame this problem: it encrypted a list of popular passwords and compared them with encrypted passwords in the password file that was accessible to anyone.

Comparing UNIX System V Release 4 to the UNIX version that the Internet worm successfully 'used', they differ in that the password file under UNIX System V Release 4 is not readable for any user. You are protected from worms the same way you are protected from unauthorized access to the system. The most important security measure is the careful choice of a password. If your system and your login account are well protected from unauthorized break-ins, then you will also be secure against an invasion of worms.

In addition, you should be careful about using .rhosts files, which are used to set up trusted hosts. Worms could get into the trusted hosts without providing a password. Trust is an ideal environment for worms and their propagation. The same is true for .netrc files, set up to facilitate file transfer with the ftp command. Never use .netrc files, if you don't want to compromise the security of your system!

2.8.4   Trojan horses

Trojan horses are programs that seem to function normally and produce the exact results that the program user intended; they have, however, damaging side-effects. One example of a Trojan horse is as follows:

A programmer writes a program for a bank that registers the interest earned by bank customers. The program is supposed to compute the interest to the thousandth, that is, three digits to the right of the decimal point. The programmer implements the program so that it books the correct total interest in cents to the customers' accounts, but the remaining tenths of cents are deposited in his own account.

Other Trojan horses can reformat the hard disk, or change or delete files. Trojan horses are the most common type of malicious program found on UNIX systems.

Trojan horses do not have to be compiled programs. PostScript files, editor buffers, *awk*, *sed* or shell scripts can contain Trojan horses. For example, at some point in a seemingly useful shell script, the following commands could be included:

```
rm -rf $HOME
echo Boooooom!
```

When an unsuspecting user starts the shell procedure, the user's home directory will be deleted and the screen will show the 'message'

```
Boooooom!
```

To avoid Trojan horses, check all programs, shell procedures, and other executable files on your system for side-effects of this kind. At the very least, you should be extremely careful with programs of unknown origins. In addition, never run a program under the user login root unless it is absolutely necessary. A user logged in as *root* who executes the example 'Trojan shell script' can destroy the entire file system. The first time you execute a program or script, you should do it in a very restricted environment. This will limit the damage resulting from a Trojan horse. For this purpose, you can use the system call *chroot(2)*.

2.8.5   Logic bombs

Logic bombs are so named because they are programmed to work like time bombs. They are inserted in programs that for a time perform correctly. However, the program has been designed so that at some point, dependent on the time or on some condition, the program begins executing illegal or damaging actions: it deletes files, causes the system to crash or does other damage. For example, depending on how it is designed, a logic bomb can be set off by a user logging in to the system, the execution of a certain program, or by a certain time and date.

You can protect against logic bombs by testing thoroughly any program you want to install. To protect against loss of data generally, you should make backups of your files regularly.

2.8.6 Back doors and trap doors

A so-called back door or trap door gives a user access to the system without the normal identification and authentification procedure that is otherwise required. Using a trap door someone can gain access without giving a user name and password. Often trap doors develop accidentally without malicious intent, later leading to possibly disastrous results. Most trap doors are written by programmers as part of application programs or operating systems, used to ease debugging and testing of the program.

The Internet worm of November, 1988 spread by making use of a trap door – the DEBUG option of the *sendmail* in that version of UNIX. After testing of the program was finished, the trap door was inadvertently left, so that the released version also had the trap door: it was possible to use it to gain access to the system from a remote machine without having to give a user name and password. Another kind of trap door is created by unauthorized users who have managed to break into a system, so-called hackers. Once in, such intruders will change a password, creating a trap door for themselves so that they can get into the system unhindered again and again.

To secure your system against trap doors, the same guidelines should be followed as against Trojan horses: test new software that you want to install. Whenever possible, you should inspect the source code and review its implemented functionality carefully before installing it. Use only programs that come from a trustworthy source.

Chapter 3
System administration

As the system administrator, you have the main responsibility for ensuring that your UNIX system is as secure as possible. If you are responsible for an enhanced UNIX system meeting special security requirements, you take on even more responsibility for a secure system in the role of 'security administrator'. The following tasks are included in the responsibilities:

- administration of access permissions on a UNIX system

- administration of user login accounts

- administration of data archives

- administration of communication services

- uncovering breaches of system security

Whenever possible, use the system administrator menu interface provided with your UNIX system. In addition, you are responsible for the security of networked systems.

3.1 Installing and configuring your system

Before you begin installing the UNIX system, you should carefully plan the configuration of your system. Write down what tasks are to be completed and how they are to be accomplished. This way you can get the system operational as quickly as possible, avoiding mistakes, and have a written record of the actions you took while installing and configuring the system. After you have completed your plan, carry it out, and as you do, record any deviation from the original plan.

The only active terminal when the system is booted is the console, which is referred to through the device file */dev/term/tty000*, or */dev/term/ttylc*. All system messages are output to this terminal. Frequently, messages output to the console are relevant to system security. For that reason, access to the console should be reserved for the system administrator; other users should not have access to it. Make the console the only terminal where the users *root* or *admin* can log in. You can do this by setting the following entry in the file */etc/default/login*:

```
CONSOLE=/dev/console
```

In addition, an important key to keeping your UNIX system secure is to keep physical access to the UNIX machine limited to the system administrator only, in particular access to the floppy drives. An intruder can illegally get system administrator privileges: to do this he can shut off the machine and reboot it using UNIX installation floppies. To prevent this type of break-in, you should lock the floppy drives or keep the machine in a locked room. In addition, the installation floppies should only be accessible to the system administrator.

Using the command *mount* you mount the device files for hard disks and external file systems. The directory in which a file system is mounted is called the 'mount point'. When you have mounted the file system, the mount point gets the same access permissions and owner as are in force for the root directory of the mounted directory. If you want to mount a file system for which users should have only read permissions, use *mount* with the option –*r*.

When users request the mounting of 'private' file systems, check whether the file system contains s-bit programs. Mount the file system in a directory that can only be searched by *root*. Remove the s-bits from the files that belong to the user. Unmount the file system and mount it again at the final location.

3.2   User administration

To avoid any inconsistencies in user attributes, always use the menu interface to set up a new user login account. You should use the shell command only if your UNIX system has no administration menu interface that automates tasks such as adding new users. Use of such an interface reduces errors which could result in a non-secure state of the UNIX system. By filling in the menu forms using the system administrator account *admin* or *root*, you change the password files */etc/passwd* and */etc/shadow*, create a login directory and a login shell for the new user and assign the user to a group.

3.2.1   Creating user groups

To add a new user, you must first add the user group to which the new user will be assigned membership. You can also assign the user to a group that has already been created.

The creation of a new user group must be done using the menu. If your system has no system administration menu, you can use the *groupadd* command:

```
# /usr/sbin/groupadd -g 500 project
```

This is how a group called *project* with the group ID number *500* is created. A user can belong to more than one group. Put users together in groups that are working on a common project or in one department. If one user needs to be separated from all others, then for that user you can create a one-member group. Every user must belong to at least one user group. In the password file */etc/passwd*, a group number must be given for each user. Every group number referenced in */etc/passwd* must be defined in the group file */etc/group*. Do not use group passwords.

3.2.2   Assigning user login accounts

After you set up a user group for a new user, you can define the user login account. To set up a new user login account, use the command *useradd*:

```
# useradd -u 301 -g 500 -d /home/peter -s
/usr/bin/sh -m peter
```

In the example, the user login account *peter* is created. The user number (UID) for the new user is *301*, the group number (GID) is *500*. The home directory for *peter* is set to */home/peter*. The login shell for *peter* is the Bourne shell, */usr/bin/sh*.

Instead of the user's first or last name, the user name should use abbreviations that cannot be found in any dictionary. This will make it somewhat harder to guess the login name.

The user ID number serves to classify processes and files as belonging to that user, the owner, who is also identified with the user name. If a user ID number is accidentally assigned to more than one user, all those users will have the same access to the files that were created under that user ID. In this way, a user *peter* could have access to the user *michael*'s files because the two have the same user ID.

The directory */etc/skel* contains the standard file *.profile*, which is automatically copied to the new user's home directory:

```
# cat /etc/skel/.profile
#       This is the default standard profile pro-
vided to a user.
#       They are expected to edit it to meet their
own needs.
MAIL=/usr/mail/${LOGNAME:?}
PATH=$PATH:/usr/ucb:/opt/bin
#
```

To make new accounts more secure, add the following settings to the file /etc/skel/.profile:

```
umask 077
mesg n
```

As long as the user does not alter these entries, you ensure that any files created by the user will then be accessible only to the user. And, to prevent manipulation of the terminal, the user prevents the terminal from receiving *write* messages.

3.2.3   Assigning passwords

Your UNIX system has two password files: /etc/passwd and /etc/shadow. The system uses the file /etc/passwd to identify every user. It contains

- the user name
- the user ID number
- the group ID number
- the home directory
- the user's login shell

as well as comments about each user.

You can define some password characteristics in the file /etc/default/passwd, using the following variables:

PASSLENGTH	for the minimum length of a password
MINWEEKS	for the minimum number of weeks, during which the password may not be changed
MAXWEEKS	for the maximum number of weeks a password can remain unchanged before the user is required to change it
WARNWEEKS	for the number of weeks before the password expires that a warning message will be sent to the user

The file *letc/shadow* contains the encrypted password of each user and information about expiry of the password. The file *letc/shadow* can only be read by the system administrator.

To give a new user a temporary password, use the command *passwd*:

```
# passwd -f peter
```

When you use this command, make sure that the user, in this case *peter*, immediately changes the password. At the prompt *New password*: enter the temporary password. You will then get the prompt *Re-enter new password*: and the temporary password must be entered again.

3.2.4   Administering passwords

Without exception, assign a password to every user account and to system login accounts such as *root, admin, uucp, shutdown, daemon* or *sys*. Tell the new user what the assigned password is and instruct them to change the password immediately.

The command *passwd* gives you the capability to set time requirements on passwords. When 'password ageing' is used, the password will expire after the specified amount of time and the user will be forced to change the password. To set up password ageing, use the *passwd* options:

−n   to give the minimum *min* number of days that must elapse between password changes

−x   to give the maximum *max* number of days before a password expires

−w   to give the number of days before the password will expire that the user should get a warning

There is a danger that accompanies password ageing: again and again the user is forced to think up a password that is difficult to guess. Not all users are going to be able to invent an effective password right away every time they get the message on their terminal:

```
Your password has expired. Choose a new one
```

Even if the user chooses a suitable password, it isn't certain that all following password changes will produce non-trivial passwords. Many users, forced by password ageing to change their passwords periodically, simply switch back and forth between two passwords.

In spite of these drawbacks, if you still want to use password ageing, you should give the users time to come up with a good new password. Therefore, warn users a certain amount of time before the old passwords expire that they need to invent a new password.

For system security, getting users to use 'secure' passwords is more important than password ageing. Make sure that users are informed about what constitutes good passwords and what passwords are not suitable. In Chapter 2 you can find complete information about this in Section 2.3.2.

3.2.5   Temporary user login accounts

Many UNIX systems have a login account *guest*, which can be used by those who do not belong to the department or organization that owns the system. Such 'guests', who need system access only temporarily, should be treated just as other users are treated. Thus instead of the user login *guest*, individual user login accounts should be furnished for each individual guest. This is the only way you can later determine which user violated system security. Otherwise, anonymous user logins like *guest* cannot be identified with one particular user. As soon as a guest no longer needs to work on the system, block the user login account.

3.2.6   Blocking a user account

You have two methods to use for blocking a user login:

- you block the account using the menu interface for system administrators
- you block the account using shell commands

You can also block an account by changing its expiry date. To do this, you can use the command *usermod* with the option *–e*, with which you can set the expiry data of the user login account. So, if you would like to set the account *peter* to expire on August 5, 1994, you can use the following command:

```
$ usermod -e 8/5/94
$
```

An input of *usermod –e" "* cancels the effect of the expiry date.

3.2.7   Removing user accounts and groups

Remove a user login account when the user no longer needs access to the system. This reduces the risk that some unauthorized person will be able to break in to the system:

```
$ find / -user peter -ok rm -rf {}\;
```

The option *–ok* in the *find* command indicates that you want to be prompted for confirmation before each deletion.

To delete a user login account, you can use the menu interface, or the command *userdel*. For example, to delete the account *peter*, enter the following command:

```
$ userdel -r peter
$
```

This will remove the user login account *peter* and delete its home directory from the system.

To delete a group, use the command *groupdel*. First, make sure that there are no more files belonging to the group you will be deleting. For example, if you are going to delete the group *project*, search for files with the group *project*:

```
$ find / -group project -print
```

Check all the files found and decide whether each should be deleted or assigned to another group. Then delete the group:

```
# groupdel project
```

You have deleted the entry for *project* from the file */etc/group*. You are restricted from editing system files such as */etc/shadow*, */etc/passwd* or */etc/group*. To change these files, always use the appropriate commands *usermod*, *useradd*, *userdel*, *groupmod*, *groupadd* or *groupdel*.

If you find files with *ls –l* that have a number instead of a group name, these are files for which the group no longer exists.

3.3   Administration of device files

For every device connected to the computer, there is a device file. The device files are stored in the directory */dev* or in one of the subdirectories of */dev*. For an overview of device files, see your UNIX documentation.

Some application programs (especially databases) need direct access to a hard disk sector, also called a 'slice'. In such cases, the device file for a hard disk slice must be readable and writable. The hard disk slice should be reserved exclusively for the program.

Moreover, you should ensure that the access permissions on device files are the minimum permissions necessary for non-privileged users to be able to work with them. This means that only the user *root* should have read and write privileges for slices of the hard disk and the corresponding device files in */dev/dsk* and */dev/rdsk*. If users have read permissions for a hard disk slice, they can use a program to read all files that are stored on the hard disk slice. With write privileges for the device file of a hard disk slice, users can even delete the files. On

Berkeley systems, access to devices often depends on the permissions for the *group* that is allowed to read from or write to the device. Programs are then given the s-bit to (temporarily) grant the permissions of *group*.

Before you create device files with the command *mknod*, you should use *umask 077* to ensure that only the user *root* will get read and write permissions for the files created. For example, here is how you could create a device file for a terminal:

```
$ umask 077
$ /sbin/mknod /dev/term/tty007 c 12 7
$ ls -l /dev/tty007
crw------- 1 root    root        12, 7  Dec 21
8:47  /dev/term/tty007
$
```

3.4   Monitoring security

In order to recognize security violations, periodically (for instance, monthly) you must check your system. There are several commands and programs you can use to determine where your system has security problems. If you suspect that unauthorized users are attempting to gain access to your system, you should immediately initiate audits and defensive precautions.

3.4.1   Checking user logins

When you are checking user logins, look out for which users have access to the system, which login accounts are necessary, and which accounts should be blocked or deleted. Make sure all accounts are protected with a password:

```
# grep '^[^:]*::' /etc/shadow
```

Using this command you will get a listing of all lines of the file */etc/shadow* which have an empty password field.

Check the login directory of each user, looking for access permissions on files and directories that give other users more permissions than they need for their shared work. Look for security deficiencies in the user's *.profile* (see Chapter 2).

Use *find* to search the user's directories for s-bit programs:

```
# find / -perm -4000 -o -perm -2000 -print
```

This command will find the files which have the s-bit set for the owner (*–perm –4000*) or for the group (*–perm –2000*). If you find s-bit programs, you could decide that you can avoid using them by creating a new group. This is because s-bits are used in most cases to give other users the same permissions for certain objects as the owner has. In most cases, if the owner of the objects and the other users of the objects are in a group together, the owner's program will not have to have the s-bit set.

Alternatively, you can use

```
# ncheck -F file system type -s
```

to get a list of all s-bit programs within the file system *file system*.

If the user's directories contain programs belonging to other users that have the s-bit set, tell the user concerned that these programs should be checked. S-bit programs that belong to you should not be in any other user's directories.

Make sure that the files */etc/passwd* and */etc/group* are owned by the user *root* and that other users are allowed only read permission for those files. Normally, the encrypted password file */etc/shadow* is only readable for *root*. Use *ls –l* to check the access permissions and the owner of the password files. Your entries must be correct and consist of:

- seven fields in the file */etc/passwd*
- three fields in the file */etc/shadow*
- four fields in the file */etc/group*

that are separated by colons. You can use the command *pwck* to check for the correct number of fields, the user name, user ID, and group ID of the password file */etc/passwd*. The *pwck* command also checks if the login directory is present and whether all programs needed by the login shell are available. The command *grpck* similarly checks the accuracy of the entries in the group file */etc/group*.

You can use a program to search for passwords that are easy to guess. Such a program, called a *password cracker*, uses an internal list of 'insecure' passwords, as well as a list you create yourself. See Chapter 2 for information about what comprises insecure passwords.

3.4.2   Monitoring user activity

In addition to your periodic check on system security, you should randomly monitor the users' activities. In the intervals between the regular security checks, the user cannot be allowed to assume that security violations and unauthorized actions will go undiscovered. There are several commands that you can use to check the status of the system security.

who

The command *who* informs you about which users are logged in to the system, for how long and on what terminal. Generally, *who* gets its information from the file */usr/adm/utmp*, which stores only a record of logins and logouts that have taken place in the very recent past. Using the command

$ **who /usr/adm/wtmp**

you can get a more complete history about logins, logouts and system crashes.

You should use *who* frequently to get a picture of the regular user activity and to register any unusual activity. After a while, you get to know which users are logged on the system every day, which users are on at specific times and on certain days (that is, only days, evenings, nights, weekends). If *who* tells you about unusual user activity, it can be a break-in to the system, for example if a user who is currently ill or on vacation is shown to be logged in, or if a user who normally works only in the evenings or at night is logged in during the morning.

When intruders log in as authorized system users, you can recognize the disguise by the unusual login time. You should also be suspicious when you see from *who* that a user did not log out at the end of the day and has remained logged in for more than a day. During the intervals when the user is not present, an unauthorized user could abuse the login at the legitimate user's terminal.

ps

Another command for monitoring user activity is *ps*. Use *ps* to determine which processes require large amounts of time, running for hours or days, and which users are running many processes simultaneously. Observe the users' processes often enough to get an impression of the normal activity. What commands are preferred by which users? If you get to know the usual activity of the authorized users, you will notice any unusual activity that could suggest illegal actions.

whodo

The command *whodo* combines the functionality of the commands *who* and *ps*. They show you how many times a user is logged in, from which terminal, and when each login session began. In addition, for every login session, you get the time of the last input, the run time consumed by its processes and the run time so far by the process that is currently active.

last

With the command *last* you can get information about the times of users' last logins and logouts and which terminal was used. If the user had logged in from another system, it also tells the name of the remote machine. Normally, *last* outputs a record of login activity in descending order. If you give a user name as argument to *last*, it will return only the login activity times of that user. The command also indicates whether the user is still logged in or if the session was terminated after a *reboot*.

For example, if the user *peter* wants to know whether other users have used his terminal *tty007*, he can enter

```
$ last tty007
```

and get the output

```
peter     tty007    Fri Aug  3  15:53     still
logged in
paul      tty007    Fri Aug  3  13:13  -  14:31
   (01:18)
michael tty007    Wed Aug  1  23:32     still
logged in
```

acctcom

The command *acctcom* will give you information about processes that have already terminated, in contrast to *ps*, which gives you current process activity. The *acctcom* command gives you the user login which started the process, the terminal that controlled it, the times it started and finished, the process's total run time, and memory usage. Here also it is important to become familiar with the pattern of normal system activity, so that you can easily recognize unusual activity that indicates a potential violation of system security. You should especially take note of processes that belong to the user *root*, and of *login* processes. Such processes could indicate that someone is attempting to break into the system or that a user got the *root* privileges without authorization.

History record files

UNIX creates history files, in which it records user activities that are issues for system security. The file */usr/adm/wtmp* contains a record of all logins in binary format. You can look at */usr/adm/wtmp* by using the command *who /usr/adm/wtmp*. It outputs a list of user names, the terminal, the date, and the time of the login:

```
huber term/tty024    Jan 26 10:17
      term/tty024    Jan 26 11:39
guest term/tty022    Jan 26 12:14
meier term/tty007    Jan 26 12:17
sauer term/tty002    Jan 26 13:03
```

The time of each user's last login is registered in the binary file */usr/adm/lastlog*. The data in */usr/adm/lastlog* is printed every time a user logs in:

```
login: peter
password:
Last login: Mon Jan 25  13:18:59 from sfsup
```

The command *finger* can also show the time of the last login. The file does not have a record of the last login using */sbin/su*.

The file */usr/adm/sulog* is a record of all attempts to use the command */sbin/su*. The data included in the file are the date, time, the user name, and the terminal where the attempt was initiated:

```
$ cat /usr/adm/sulog
SU 04/07 10:34 + term/tty002 huber-meier
SU 04/08 02:21 - term/tty021 guest-root
SU 04/08 02:23 - term/tty021 guest-root
```

The example shows that a user in the user account *guest* tried to log in unsuccessfully twice using */sbin/su*. Failed attempts are shown with –.

You can install a program package for monitoring user activities that influence the security of your UNIX system. Using such an audit system, you can keep records of the user, time, the object, and the success of user actions that affect system security. The fact that an audit system is monitoring your UNIX system has the effect of frightening off users who might have tried to perform unauthorized actions.

3.5   Data backup and restore

To reduce the risk of data loss owing to hardware problems or human error, your system's data should be backed up to external storage media at regular intervals.

Store the media backup copies so that they are well protected from unauthorized access or theft.

Make sure that you will be able to use the backup copy to reconstruct lost data on another system. For this purpose, back up files using relative pathnames which will work on any UNIX system, instead of absolute pathnames specific to one particular system.

Make a full system backup immediately after you install the system (see also the *System Administrator's Guide*). This will enable you to recover the UNIX-partition (slice 0) data quickly if your hard disk fails. User data is not backed up in a system backup.

Use the command *ufsdump* to back up user data. This command backs up either all files of the file system or all files that have changed since a given date. There are 10 different backup levels (0 to 9). The files backed up will be all the files of the file system that have changed since the last *ufsdump* backup with a lower backup level.

For example, every Tuesday a level 2 backup is performed, followed by a level 4 backup on Wednesday, then on Thursday a level 3 backup will back up all files that are new or have changed since the level 2 backup from Tuesday. A backup of level 0 backs up the entire file system.

The following shows how to perform a backup of slice 4 (*/home*) onto a 150 MB magnetic tape:

```
# init s
# killall
# fsck -F ufs /dev/rdsk/c0d0s4
# ufsdump -0usf 9000 /dev/rdsk/c0d0s4
```

The options used here are:

0   backup level 'complete backup'

u   date of the backup will be recorded in the file /etc/dumpdates

s   capacity of the data media (tape length: 9000 feet corresponds to 150 MB)

f   the target file (usually the device file of the tape drive)

To restore the user data, use the command *ufsrestore*:

```
# cd /home
# ufsrestore rf /dev/rmt/c0s0
```

Before a new installation, you can use the menu interface to back up the local configuration and user logins.

The commands *cpio*, *tar*, or *dd* are sufficient for backups of smaller amounts of data.

The command *cpio* can be used to exchange and back up data. In this example, the data is backed up to a floppy:

```
$ ls | cpio -ovc > /dev/rdsk/f0t
```

Using *dd*, you can copy and convert files, as well as physically copy complete UNIX slices. If the slice is not too large, it can also be copied to magnetic tape:

```
# init 1
# killall
# umountall
# fsck -F ufs /dev/rdsk/c0s0
# dd if=/dev/rdsk/c0d0s4 of=/dev/rdsk/c0s0
# dd if=/dev/rdsk/c0d0s4 of=/dev/rdsk/c0d1s4
#
```

3.6 Network administration

The security of networked UNIX systems depends on how well the communication functions of each system are protected from abuse and error. UNIX systems use the communication systems UUCP, TCP/IP and NFS. The following section sketches the security problems of UUCP in particular. A complete discussion of system security in networks could fill its own book and is beyond the intended scope of this book.

3.6.1   uucp

Generally you should not view any *uucp* system as secure. After a remote user logs in to the local system, *uucp* will let the user work completely unrestricted, unless you do something to prevent it. To provide security of the *uucp* system, be sure to take the following steps:

- Create an individual user login account for each remote machine that is allowed to connect to your system via *uucp*.
- Under UNIX System V Release 3 and all the following releases of UNIX System V, fill in the entries in the file */etc/uucp/Permissions* so that each system gets only the access permissions needed to be able to complete the tasks for which the remote communication is necessary. You control the access permissions with the option *LOGNAME* in the file */etc/uucp/Permissions*. You assign *LOGNAME* the authorized user logins and can control the access allowed to these accounts with a variety of options:

  - *LOGNAME*=user_logins options
  - *LOGNAME* tells which user names from remote systems are allowed to log in to the local system, for instance, the user login names *peter*, *michael* and *maria*:
  - *LOGNAME*=maria:michael:peter
    The options determine the access permissions allowed to those users. The entry *LOGNAME* tells that all user logins are allowed, unless they are excluded using another entry.

  There are further options:

  - *WRITE*=directory
    This option tells which part of the file system can be accessed for write. The standard setting for this option is *WRITE=/usr/spool/uucp-public*.
  - *READ*=directory
    This option indicates which part of the file system can be read.
  - *REQUEST*=option
    This option sets whether the remote user may have read access to local files. If the option is set to *yes*, then you are permitting read access; with *no* you disallow read access.

- *SENDFILES*=option
  The value of this option determines whether jobs for the remote machine may be processed. Again, the option set to *yes* gives permission to send files and *no* refuses permission.

- *NOWRITE*=directory
  You can use this option to reduce the writable area that you set with the option *WRITE*.

- *NOREAD*=directory
  This option reduces the readable area that you set with the option *READ*.

- *CALLBACK*=option
  The value of this option indicates whether you want to use the 'call back' function. If it is set to *yes*, the local system will answer the request of the remote system by hanging up and initiating a request to connect to the remote system.

  This is how you can ensure that connections can actually be established only with machines that are authorized to access the local machine. This prevents someone from disguising themselves as an authorized user by using an authorized login account and password from an unauthorized machine.

  The *CALLBACK* function works only in one direction. If both machines have the call back option set, when one of them attempts to establish a connection between the machines, it would start a constant cycle of each machine hanging up and calling the other back. The default setting for *CALLBACK* is *no*.

- *VALIDATE*=system name
  With this option you can set which remote machines may be used by the user logins set in *LOGNAME*.

- *PUBDIR*=directory
  This option sets the name of a directory set aside for public read and write access. The default setting for *PUBDIR* is */usr/spool/uucppublic*.

- *MYNAME*=name
  Using this option, you can change the name of the local machine for the purposes of *uucp* connections.

- *MACHINE*=name
  This option indicates that you only want to allow connection with the remote machine given. The entry *MACHINE=OTHER* says that *uucp* should be able to connect to any system unless the system is excluded via some other declaration.

If you don't have a *Permissions* file in the directory */usr/lib/uucp* (on some systems, the directory is */etc/uucp*), you will have a file USERFILE instead. In this case (for example in Berkeley UNIX versions), you must edit USERFILE to determine which files on your computer can be accessed by the UUCP system. The USERFILE entries take the form:

```
user-login-name,system-name [c] directories
```

The user-login-name in USERFILE specifies the user login name in */etc/passwd* that will be used when a remote system logs in using that user login name. By *user-login-name*, you can also determine which files on the local system may be copied via UUCP to a remote system. The letter *c* (for callback) is optional. It specifies that conversation stops after the remote system calls the local system, which then calls back the remote system, in order to prove the identity of the calling remote system. With the *directories* entry, that is, a list of absolute directory pathnames separated by blanks, you determine that remote systems can only access files in the directories specified. Without this entry, remote users can access any file in the system. A *directories* entry of '/' has the same effect.

An entry in USERFILE may look similar to this:

```
uusun,sun  c  /usr/spool/uucppublic
```

In this example, only the user *uusun* on the remote system *sun* is permitted to log in to the local system.

For systems that are only called by your system, and never log in, the user login name is not used. Instead, the system name preceded by a comma is used. Such an entry might look like the following:

```
,mars  /usr/spool/uucppublic
```

The system *mars* is called by the local system, and never logs in.

If a system or user tries to log in without an entry in USERFILE, the connection to the remote system will be terminated.

Wildcard entries keep this mechanism from working, like those delivered with many UNIX systems:

```
nuucp,  /usr/spool/uucppublic
,  /
```

There is no problem, as long as no new UUCP login is added to the file */etc/passwd*. The UUCP login *nuucp* from the file */etc/passwd* will match the first line in the USERFILE, but not the wildcard entry. But any new UUCP login will match the wildcard entry. The wildcard entry begins with a comma, permitting a system to copy files from anywhere in the local system. Since the comma entry allows local users to access UUCP-owned files and directories without restrictions, such an entry should never appear in your USERFILE.

The good news is that even with complete access granted by USERFILE, UNIX file permissions are still valid. If a user wants to copy local files to a remote system, those files must grant all users, or UUCP, the read and write permissions. Otherwise, a remote system has no access to the files or directories.

To prevent users from other computers from changing the USERFILE, don't make entries that give access to the directory */usr/lib/uucp* (or */etc/uucp*)!

3.6.2   Network services

UNIX systems offer several network services: *telnet, rlogin, rsh, mail, ftp, xhost*. Every network service involves security risks, and you will have to consider whether the advantages for the user are more important than the possible damage that could be done. If you decide that the security risks of a network service are too high, you can disable the network so that it will not be available. To disable a network service, edit the files in the directories */etc/rc1.d, /etc/rc2.d* and */etc/rc3.d*, inserting the hash sign (#) at the beginning of the lines that start the network services.

The same mechanisms for controlling access on a local system are used to control network access. To gain access to the system, users must identify themselves with user login name and password; file access is governed by the respective permissions. A user who wants to work on a local machine using the network must be entered in the file */etc/passwd*. The access permissions are given according to the user and group ID numbers in the network user's entry in */etc/passwd*.

If you do not want to allow all users data transfer capabilities via *ftp*, in the file */etc/inet/ftpusers* enter the login names of the users you want restricted from using *ftp*.

Users can log in to a remote system without entering a password, if the following conditions are met: the user has a login account on the remote machine and has set up an *.rhosts* file in the home directory of that account, containing the remote system name.

You can keep a list of machines that are 'trusted' in the file */etc/hosts.equiv*. If a user from one of the machines from the list tries to log in and their user login is listed in the password file */etc/passwd*, then the system will allow the user to log in without requiring a password.

If an unauthorized user discovers the password of a legitimate user who has the capability to log on to a remote system without giving a password, this threatens the security of the local system as well as all systems where one can log in without a password. An intruder needs only to get a user login with which he can log in to another system without a password. Then he can simply 'climb' from one system to the next. If there is a user login in system A which will also be accepted without a password on system B, the intruder will have no trouble getting into system B. If system B also has a login that allows access to system C without a password, then the path from system A to system C is clear, even though the original intent was only to allow access from A to B without a password.

In this way, an intruder, if he can get into one user login account, can get onto several remote systems.

Chapter 4
Security for programmers

4.1 Work environment
4.2 Programming guidelines

4.3 Programming X Window user
     interfaces

Every programmer of a UNIX system is at the same time a user. Thus, the recommendations to users in Chapter 2 are just as valid for programmers. Those recommendations include the choice of effective, secure passwords, allocation of access permissions and the review of the work environment to recognize potential security problems. Adding to the issues they must consider as users, this chapter deals with the security issues that are especially important for programmers.

4.1 Work environment

For a programmer a good working environment is important since it enables faster results. When developing programs that have an influence on data security, a good working environment is also important because the product results have an effect on the security of the system.

All software developers should take the following precautions to ensure the security of programming projects:

- *Assignment of personal responsibility*   This means every programmmer as 'owner' is responsible for a particular software module. Changes to a software module must be agreed upon with the owner and the owner personally implements the changes in his or her code. UNIX supports this kind of distribution of software modules to owners in that owners of data objects determine the assignment of access permissions (see Chapter 2).

- *Principles of structured programming*   The use of structured programming principles will produce program code that is easy to read and maintain. Easy maintenance is especially critical for programs that influence data security. The structured development methods SA/RT (Structured Analysis with Real-Time extensions) and SD/MD (Structured Design/Modular Design) make maintenance easier by using more modularization.

- *Group review of program design*   An individual programmer trying to find a problem may not always understand all particulars of the program and how pieces fit together, especially as they relate to data security. There can be misunderstandings, even when a program is well documented. A group review of program code can sometimes point out security issues and other problems. It helps to ensure that program design is being implemented without errors or side-effects.

Code review methods include formal inspection and Development Document Control (DDC). DDC is a written review, while formal inspection takes place at a meeting where a design document or code fragment is inspected systematically.

The term 'Formal Inspection' was introduced by M. Fagan to distinguish this type of review from more or less free-form code reviews. A formal inspection checks a document or code fragment for correctness and completeness following a set procedure that dictates the process and assigns the participants to various roles.

The goal of reviews should not simply be to find errors that affect the functionality of the program. A program can also cause side-effects that could be exploited by a malicious user to damage the confidentiality or integrity of the data. Such side-effects must be uncovered by the review process and eliminated.

- *Reproducible and documented tests for the program*   Design a set of tests that can run with as little user interaction as possible. Establish definitive test result expectations: exactly what will be acceptable as a success and what constitutes failure. As well as testing the program as a whole, also develop tests for the individual program modules.

- *Version control*   Use a control system such as SCCS (Source Code Control System) that manages source code versions. SCCS supports the administration of software projects by assigning software modules and changes to a programmer who then 'owns' the code. SCCS keeps track of all changes, making it possible to reconstruct any past version of the program. If a program is changed in such a way that it causes data security to be threatened, then the programmer can use the version control system to determine who is responsible for the change.

- *Controlling the assignment of access permissions even more than with normal users*   Create a working environment in which the possibility of abuse is minimized. Such a working environment could consist of a limited subsystem.

Programs should be written so that they can be tested with data that has no effect on system security. You should also be able to test without having to use special privileges (for example, set user-id and set group-id). Start testing with privileges only after the code has been reviewed and the security functionality of the new program has been accepted by all the participants of your organization.

4.2 Programming guidelines

The following guidelines should be followed by programs that use shared resources. Security problems can result if a program can access a resource when it should not be able to get the appropriate permission. Because of an overload of resource requests, the result could be that other users cannot access their own data.

4.2.1 Evaluation of return values from system calls

Programmers should ensure that every request for system services results in a message indicating that the request was carried out successfully. If the request failed the programmer should be asking the questions:

- Does the user need to be informed of the failure?
- Does the failure affect the security of the program or system? Should a record of the failure be written to a protocol file?
- Can program execution proceed in spite of the failure? Should the program retry the action that failed?

The answers often depend on the error types: the programmer makes error handling dependent on return values, taking a separate action in each individual case.
There can be several reasons why a program executes with errors:

- Privileged functions make system calls such as *chroot()* which itself could fail on calls to other functions. For this reason it is possible to execute the function without having to have its privileges. The program must be able to recognize such a case and exit without errors, even if the user's request has not been executed.
- The *fork()* system call can result in an error if it fails to create a new process because space is unavailable in memory or in the process table. The return value of *fork()* indicates the parent process (result > 0) or the child process (result = 0). Often, programs don't check for a negative return value, the error condition.

```
/* Example of incomplete code */

int pid;
...
```

```
if ((pid = fork()) == 0) {
  /* child process code */
  ...
  exit(0);
}
/* parent process code */
...
```

In this example the parent process executes regardless of whether *fork()* was successful. It checks only whether *fork()* returns the value 0. However, *fork()* could return an error condition indicating that, for whatever reason, it had failed to create a child process.

The following example checks the *fork()* return value correctly:

```
/* Complete example, checking all conditions */

int pid
...
switch (pid = fork()) {
case 0:
    /* child process code*/
    ...
    break;
case -1;
    /* code for error condition */
    ...
    break;
default:
    /* parent process code */
    ...
    break;
}
```

- Programs should also respond to errors that currently seem not to be probable. Code changes during the lifetime of the program could facilitate the emergence of such errors.

- Using the global variable *errno*, programs can determine more about the causes of errors. Using *errno* can enable the program to respond correctly to errors and provide the user with helpful error messages.

4.2.2   Portable program code

In UNIX systems, various system size limits are defined using symbolic constants. Your programs should always use these symbolic constants as opposed to absolute values which are valid only for the specific UNIX system you are using. Otherwise, when these values differ in individual versions of the operating system, the correctness and security of the program could be at risk.

For example: at a certain time, you want to be sure that all files will be closed. The maximum number of open files allowed per process is defined by the symbolic constant *OPEN_MAX*:

```
for (fd = 0; fd < OPEN_MAX; fd++)
    (void) close(fd);
```

It doesn't matter whether the constant *OPEN_MAX* has the value 20, 25, or 35. Perhaps you used the value 20 instead of the symbolic constant because in your system *OPEN_MAX* is assigned that value. This causes problems when you run the program on a newer UNIX system or on some other system. If, on the other system, *OPEN_MAX* is defined with the value 35, then the sample program will only close the first 20 files. The remaining 15 will not be closed, so the original intent of the program will not be accomplished.

4.2.3   Programming environment

Most programs operate under some assumptions concerning the language version, compiler, processor, and available instruction set, which could differ depending on the specific implementation. At the beginning of your programs, you should have tests checking that all assumptions are in fact true. If one or more of the assumed conditions are not met, the program should output an error message.

Assumptions about the calling environment must be tested as well. So, for example, the program should test signal handling functions, the default access permissions set with *umask*(), and check the files that are to be opened.

You should give up any privileges you don't need. The executable file of the program could have the set-user-ID attribute set, when the program doesn't actually need set-user-ID privileges. In such a situation, the program should begin with instructions that turn off its unnecessary privileges; you can use the system call *setuid*() to set the effective user ID back to the real user ID:

```
retcode = setuid (getuid());
```

4.2.4   Programmer discipline

Your organization must be able to guarantee the integrity of its software components well into the future. For this reason the programmer should keep in mind that the code written now will be maintained by others later. Document your program design. Comment your source code thoroughly. Design and write your programs so that future changes and maintenance will not be difficult.

Programmer discipline is not only necessary during initial development of a program; it is required for the life of a software product. Therefore, every change to the program's source code should include changes to the design documentation, in-line program documentation, and the change record.

4.2.5   Program assignment of access permissions

Ensure that all the files created by your programs get only those access rights necessary for the program to function correctly. They should not simply take on the bit mask of the process or its user and group ID numbers. Make use of the system calls *chmod()*, *chown()* and *chgrp()*, to explicitly assign the owner, group and permissions. Files that serve simply as data backup and restore buffers should not have more permissions than the files where the data is permanently stored.

4.2.6   Multitasking

In a multitasking system like UNIX, two or more users can execute the same program concurrently. Thus, it is possible that two processes could access the same file concurrently. Keep this in mind when you decide the order of file access. Most files accessed by processes are not supposed to be changed. For such a file, there is no need for any special planning for the access order. Both processes will have read access only and this does not cause any problems when the processes are reading the file at the same time.

4.2.7   Locking files

If it is necessary for a process to change a file, other processes should not easily be allowed to read or write to the file. If a process is allowed read access without consideration of parallel processes, then it could read in a version of the file that is no longer valid because another process has made some change to it. This can lead to data inconsistencies and bugs. Furthermore, two processes, both wanting to write to the same file simultaneously, can obstruct each other.

There is a simple method for avoiding such inconsistencies: for every process that writes changes to a file, make an individual copy available. When the changes are complete, each process uses the system call *link()* to create a reference so that the old filename points to the new one.

As a better alternative to the simple locking method using *link()*, you can use the C library function *lockf()* to lock whole files or data areas of files. This function reserves write access for the calling process on all or a given part of a file, denying all other processes write access to that data area. This method functions only if the participating processes coordinate file access with *lockf()*.

4.2.8   Locking data areas

The system call *fcntl()* makes sure that only one process can access a data area of
a file at one time. All other processes will be prevented from reading or writing
to the locked data area:

```
/*
 * Example of file locking using fcntl
 */
#include <sys/types.h>
#include <unistd.h>
#include <fcntl.h>
#include <stdio.h>
main(argc,argv)
int argc;
char *argv[];
{
  int        fd;
  struct  flock  lck;

  if  (argc != 2) {
    fprintf(stderr,
      "Usage: %s filename \n", argv[0]);
    exit(1);
  }

  /* Open the file for read */
  if  ((fd = open(argv[argc - 1]);
    fprintf(stderr, "%s: Cannot open %s \n",
      argv[0],  argv[argc - 1]);
        }
  /* Set the position and size of the area to be
locked */
  /* offset from the beginning of the file */
  lck.l_whence = SEEK_SET;
  lck.l_start = (off_t) 2;
  lck.l_len = (off_t) 10;

  /* Lock the area */
  lck.l_type = F_RDLCK;
  fcntl(fd,F_SETLK,&lck);

  /* read the locked area */
  ...
  /* free the locked area */
  lck.l_type = F_UNLCK;
  fcntl(fd,F_SETLK,&lck);
}
```

4.2.9   Freeing file locks

File locking also affects system security. If a program crashes or otherwise ends abnormally and still has locked files, it could affect many users who would be unable to continue work because their processing is dependent on access to the locked files. For this reason it is important that programs which lock files should test the return values of every system call, ensuring that all locks are removed as soon as they are no longer needed by the program.

By making use of temporary files in your program, you can ease the freeing of file locks in cases where the program has ended abnormally. You can remove the temporary copies by hand or change links. If your program locks individual data sets, you must find the failing process and end it with *kill*().

4.2.10   Deadlock situations

Programs that affect system security should be designed to avoid deadlock. One recommended method is for the program to lock all the necessary files before beginning any task to be executed. If deadlock occurs, it is possible to fix the problem using *kill*().

By creating a child process with *fork*(), your program can recognize and handle deadlock situations. The child process sets the locks, executes the critical functions and frees the locks. In the meantime, the parent determines, using a *timeout*, the time interval in which the child should finish its work. If the child does not finish in the time allowed, it has deadlocked and the parent can eliminate it with *kill*().

4.2.11   Child processes

Using the system call *fork*( ), a program can produce a child process. It executes in parallel with the parent process and is given a copy of the parent process environment.

A parent process often opens files to use for communicating with the child process. Child processes inherit all the opened files of the parent process and can use these files just as the parent can. Before the call to *fork*( ), a process should close all the files that the child process will not need.

Different programs can also use this method to communicate. If the parent starts these programs using one of the *exec*( ) family of system calls, they are connected and the child has access to all the open files that the parent had before the *exec*( ).

Before a call to *exec*( ), a process should close all files that are not needed by the other program. Instead of closing files explicitly before the call to *exec*(), you can use the call *fcntl*( ) to set the so-called '*close-on-exec* bit' (FD_CLOEXEC). If this bit is set, the files indicated will be closed on a call to *exec*( ).

The process environment created by the exec system call could differ from that of the original process. With the *exec()* system calls

execle()

execve()

execvpe()

execvle()

the environment of the child process can be altered.

If a program is related to another via an *exec* system call, the process environment of the newly created process could be changed. This is a security risk in programs that do not check the process environment properly. In such a case, an incorrectly set *PATH* environment variable could direct the UNIX shell to use files from directories that the program should not be able to access at all, and thereby use a 'fake' program. In the interests of security, every program should check its process environment instead of making assumptions about it.

4.2.12   Signals

Child processes also inherit from the parent the settings for signal handling. Every program should therefore check the default settings. Child processes that are supposed to run in the background often set the attribute SIG_IGN explicitly to prevent the process from reacting to real-time events such as keyboard input.

UNIX supports 31 different signals. A list of signals is in the files */usr/include/signal.h* and */usr/include/sys/signal.h*. Table 4.1 gives an overview of signals in UNIX System V Release 4.

Table 4.1   Signals in UNIX.

Signal name	Signal number	Meaning
SIGHUP	1	hangup (connection ends when a modem or network connection is interrupted)
SIGINT	2	interrupt
SIGQUIT	3	quit
SIGILL	4	illegal instruction (not reset when caught)
SIGTRAP	5	trace trap (not reset when caught)
SIGIOT	6	IOT instruction, interrupt of input and output (on PDP-11)
SIGEMT	7	EMT instruction, interrupt of an emulation (on hardware that does not support floating point)
SIGFPE	8	floating point exception
SIGKILL	9	kill (unconditonal process interrupt)
SIGBUS	10	bus error (invalid memory access, such as attempting to read a word starting off a word boundary)
SIGSEGV	11	segmentation violation (invalid memory access, such as attempting to read at an address without using the process address conversion table)
SIGSYS	12	bad argument to system call
SIGPIPE	13	attempt to write to a pipe with no one to read it
SIGALRM	14	alarm clock
SIGTERM	15	program termination
SIGURG	16	urgent termination of interrupt
SIGSTOP	17	process termination
SIGSTP	18	termination signal originating from the keyboard
SIGCONT	19	continue after termination
SIGCHLD	20	return value of a child process has changed
SIGTTIN	21	attempt to read data from a terminal when the process is running in the background
SIGTTOU	22	attempt to write data to a terminal when the process is running in the background
SIGIO	23	input or output event
SIGXCPU	24	CPU time limit expired
SIGXFSZ	25	maximum file size exceded
SIGVTALRM	26	virtual alarm clock error
SIGPROF	27	workload clock error
SIGWINCH	28	tty-window size changed
SIGUSR1	30	user defined signal 1
SIGUSR2	31	user defined signal 2

The following example shows how a program's environment can be reset:

```
#include <stdio.h>
#include <signal.h>
#include <stdlib.h>
#include <unistd.h>
```

```
#include <sys/types.h>
#include <sys/stat.h>
main (argc, argv)
int argc;
char *argv[];
{
 mode_t old_mask;
 int sig, fd, max open;
 struct sigaction *sig_state;
 sigset_t set;
 /*
  * Make sure errors are written to the terminal
  */

 freopen ("/dev/tty", "w", stderr);
 /*
  * Quit if the highest signal number
  * is not defined
  */
#ifndef NSIG
fprintf (stderr, "NSIG undefined \n");
exit (1);
#else
/*
 * Allocate memory for the signal structures
 */
sig_state =
  malloc (sizeof (struct sigaction) * NSIG);
if (sig_state == NULL) {
    fprintf (stderr, "malloc failed\n");
    exit (2);
}
/*
 * Execute and test return values
 * of signal handling routines
 */
for (sig = 1; sig < NSIG; sig++)
  if (sigaction (sig, NULL,
    sig_state + sig) == -1) {
        fprintf (stderr, "invalid signal\n");
        exit (3);
    }
/*
 * Close all files that do not
 * have to remain open
 */
```

```
     max_open = (int) sysconf (_SC_OPEN_MAX);
     for (fd = 0; fd < max_open; fd++)
        if ((fd != fileno(stdin)) &&
            (fd != fileno(stdout)) &&
            (fd != fileno(stderr)) {
            if (close(fd)) {
                 fprintf (stderr, "file cannot be
                          closed\n");
                 exit (4);
            }
        }
 }
 /*
  * Save the original permissions and reset
  * to the more secure settings
  */
 old_mask = umask(~(S_IRWXG | S_IRWXO));

 /*
  The rest of the program code follows
  */
  #endif
 }
```

4.2.13   Process communication

Using signals is the best communication method between processes that have not inherited open files via *fork*() or *exec*(). Every process is allowed to send signals to any other process, indicating that the recipient should take some action. That is an example of one-way communication.

Some conditions must be met before a process can send a signal to another. The sending process has to know the process number of the receiving process and the sender must have appropriate permission to send the recipient a signal.

The operating system also delivers signals if a recipient is not an active process. If, however, several occurrences of the same signal are supposed to be delivered to a process, it could be that the receiving process will only react once. If a signal arrives a second time before the signal handling routine has been reset, the process will terminate if 'Quit' is the default setting for that signal. To minimize this danger, you should reset the signal handling routine as soon as possible.

It is also possible that a signal will be ignored because the receiving process has ended or disabled it. In this case, you can work with a combination of signals and messages. The sending process identifies itself with a message, in which the requested service is specified. The receiving process replies by sending a signal to the sender.

Named pipes

An easier method consists of using a 'named pipe'. A named pipe is created using the system call *mknod()*. It is handled like a file, which means that processes can exchange data over named pipes. Named pipes may be allowed only the minimum access permissions necessary for process communication.

For interprocess communication via named pipes you can also use the 'FIFO device file' mechanism. With the routine *mkfifo()* you can create a device file 'FIFO'. To enable reads and writes to the file, you give it a path name and set enough access permissions to guarantee interprocess communication, but no more.

Interprocess communication

Additional means for communicating between processes are messages, semaphores for synchronization of processes and shared memory for concurrent access of the data. These communication tools comprise 'Interprocess Communication' (IPC). IPC includes provisions that enable the coordination of processes. With regard to access permissions, the IPC objects 'message', 'semaphore' and 'shared memory' behave like files. There is an owner who decides what access permissions to allow the 'group' and the 'others'.

Temporary files

Sometimes it is useful to prevent communication between processes. For this, temporary files should be created, to which other processes are denied all access, regardless of the access rights of that process.

You can use the system call *tmpfile()* to create a file. Although the name of the file will not appear in any directory, a reference to the file exists, that is, the link to the process that opened it. This process is the only one that can work with the file and no other process can get any form of access to it. The process can pass the temporary file on to another process: by using *fork()*, it is given to the child process or by using an *exec()* call, it can be passed to another program. Only when the file is closed with the system call *close()* will the file be deleted from the system completely.

4.2.14   Privileged programs

Privileged programs are programs that belong to the superuser and have the owner s-bit set. When a privileged program is started by an arbitrary user, a privileged process is created, which will have an effective user ID of 0. Because privileged programs have permissions that are not given to normal programs, it is extremely important to use caution when developing privileged programs. For such programs in particular, the 'least privilege' principle applies: a program should only get as many access permissions as are necessary to accomplish its task. Permissions that are not needed should be revoked.

In this section, privileged programs means programs that execute under a fixed effective user or group ID number. The most dangerous case is when that ID is the user ID of the system administrator. It is possible for a program to find out the user and group ID of the calling program: the system calls *getuid*() and *getgid*() return the real user and group ID of the parent program.

Using an access file you can check the real user ID and then allow continuation of program execution only for users whose real user ID is entered in the access file. If some unauthorized user calls the program, the program will not find the user ID in the access file and will terminate.

You can use the system call *access*() to check whether the calling process (user) would be allowed access to some object if the process were not privileged. The process is identified with its real user ID instead of the effective user ID. Using *access*(), a privileged program can make sure that the caller of the program is actually allowed access to the file that it wants to access. The privileged program can use the return result from *access*() to determine whether to allow file access.

Keep a record of all transactions performed by the privileged program. With the log file, you ensure that any abuse of the program can be traced. The program should store such log files in a directory that is accessible only to privileged users. Only the owner of the program should be able to access the file itself. At the very least, keep a record of when the program was called, which command was used to call it and by which user, identified by the real user ID. The log file should also be used for keeping a record of any unusual program behaviour and any violations of rules of system security.

A very important security precaution consists of keeping secret any information about the security mechanisms of a privileged program. In cases when the privileged program fails, the program should not respond with any information about why the attempt failed. Otherwise, if a potential intruder is trying to break in or abuse the program, the informative messages could help him or her to succeed.

One common example of this is authentication using the user name and password. Programs should require both user name and password before failing. If the program terminates as soon as it is determined that the user name is wrong, this tells the user which part of the input was incorrect.

Keep messages as general as possible. Such a message could read:

```
Input incorrect
```

With this, the program isn't giving away which input was incorrect.

In the program, use the s-bit privilege only as long as it is needed to complete the task. When you no longer need it, revoke the s-bit privilege with the system call *setuid*( ), setting the effective user ID number to the real user ID:

```
retcode = setuid (getuid());
```

Frequently, security problems are caused by 'indirect privileges'. This occurs when a privileged program creates a temporary file that has certain access permissions. If the privileged program has an error and teminates without deleting the temporary file, it remains and could be misused by an intruder.

It is critical to system security, then, that temporary files should be deleted if the program terminates prematurely. This is also true when the program quits because of an error. This means that the signal must be caught and that the signal handling routines should close any remaining temporary files.

It may not be possible to revoke privileges before actions that can be performed without them are taken. In this case, you can still see to it that the actions are taken without the privileges. Execute the actions as child processes that give up privileges, using the system calls *setuid()* and *setgid()*. This way, the parent process can execute all tasks that require privileges while leaving the remaining actions to be performed by child processes that are not privileged. There may also be situations where it makes sense for a non-privileged process to start a privileged process for performing tasks that require privileges. This is also a way to ensure that privileged programs only execute tasks that require privileges.

4.2.15   Shell procedures

To be able to execute a shell procedure, the user must have read permissions on the script file. Because of this, a potential intruder can look in shell procedures to find out how system security precautions are designed. This can give intruders the information that tells them how to avoid security measures or how to misuse the shell script to violate system security.

Therefore, shell procedures cannot be used for writing programs critical to system security. Such programs should be written in a compiled programming language like C. Only the compiled version of the program should be made available to non-privileged users and they should be given only execute permission for the executable file.

When you do write shell procedures, set the working environment explicitly in the script itself. There should be commands that set the search path, the default access permissions and the field separators. For example:

```
PATH=/bin:/usr/bin; export PATH
IFS=" "; export IFS
umask 077
```

Shell procedures that should only be executed by privileged users (that is, *root* and *admin*) need to record every attempted use of the program by unauthorized users:

```
# Set up working environment
PATH=/bin:/usr/bin;
IFS=" ";
export PATH IFS
umask 077
CONSOLE=/dev/console

# determine the real user
LOGNAME='realuser' # see below program "realuser"

# record any unauthorized use
if [ $LOGNAME != root -a $LOGNAME != admin ]
   then
      echo $LOGNAME is executing the program $0
           on 'tty' ! >$CONSOLE
      echo Date of the attempt: 'date' >$CONSOLE
      exit 1
fi
...
```

The program *realuser* for determining the program's real user could be written as follows:

```
#include <stdio.h>
#include <pwd.h>

main(argc, argv)
char *argv[];
{
    int r_uid;
    struct passwd *pw;
    extern struct passwd *getpwuid();

    /* get the real user ID */
    r_uid = getuid();

    /* Look for the user in the passwd file */
    pw = getpwuid(r_uid);
    if (pw == NULL)
    {
      fprintf(stderr,
              "%s: UID %d not found in the
              passwd file!\n",
              argv[0], r_uid);
      exit(1);
    }
    /* output the user's real login */
```

```
printf("%s\n", pw->pw_name);
exit(0);
}
```

Avoid giving s-bit permissions to shell files, if possible. Every s-bit can be misused by users to become *root*. Shell scripts with s-bits can be used as 'back doors' to gain unauthorized access to the system.

4.2.16   Daemons

Daemons are programs that run continuously as background processes and supply users with various system services. Typically, a daemon is started when the system is initialized and remains active until the system is brought down. The normal user cannot manipulate the execution of the program. Usually, daemons perform services that do not have to be completed immediately.

One example is the spool daemon program *lpsched*, which handles output to the printer. Working autonomously, the spool daemon checks the status of print tasks waiting in a queue. If it finds that no printer is available for a given print job, the daemon will put that task into the queue to wait until a suitable printer becomes available. So, the user does not have to wait until the print task has finished executing; instead, the print task is left for the spool daemon to process.

A normal user doesn't start the daemon itself, but a service program that initiates the communication with the daemon. The service program tells the daemon what to do, either by sending it certain files or by using other mechanisms of interprocess communication.

When you write a program that is going to execute as a daemon, you should follow the following guidelines:

- Assign access permissions with great care. Most service programs need privileges to be able to communicate with the daemon. Usually, the daemon does not need to be privileged. To make this possible, the daemon should run using the user and group ID numbers of a pseudo user account. A pseudo account serves to isolate security-sensitive programs from the rest of the UNIX system. Then the daemon can only work with objects that belong to the pseudo user account and are not accessible to any other (real) users.

- Structure the execution of the daemon. Avoid having the daemon try to do more than one task at once. After performing initializations, a daemon should process tasks in the order in which they are sent. The design structure of the program should reflect the processing of the users' tasks. A possible implementation could be structured in such a way that one task is processed during each iteration of the daemon's main program loop.

- Check the user's identity. Unlike privileged programs, a daemon cannot use *getuid*( ) to determine the real user ID of the user sending the task (the client). However, since the service program is privileged, it needs to assume this task. It should determine the real user ID of the client sending the task and then pass this information to the daemon as part of the task data.

- When a job includes files that are to be sent to the daemon, the daemon shouldn't just check the user and group of the file, since these do not necessarily have to match those of the user sending the task. So the service program needs to mark the file that is going to be processed by the daemon.

- To accomplish this, the service program should get the real user and group IDs of the client and set its own effective user and group IDs to correspond. At this point, it creates a file, and then copies into it the data to be passed on to the daemon. Now the service program can set the s-bit of the owner on the new file. Since only the owner of a file can set its s-bit, this is effectively the user's signature. Finding this 'signature', the daemon can confidently assume that the file's source is actually the user who initiated the job.

- Carefully plan the utilization of devices. Since a daemon process normally runs as long as the UNIX system does, it is important to free hardware resouces as soon as they are no longer required. If this is not done consistently, the daemon could lock up parts of the system, making them unavailable for other users. For instance, a terminal could be reserved by the daemon. As long as the daemon has control of it, no other user can use the terminal.

4.2.17   ISAM programs

The indexed sequential access method ISAM (Indexed Sequential Access Methodology) uses indices that access files. ISAM applications depend on supplemental libraries, not on system calls. In contrast to system calls, supplemental library routines do not supply the capabilities to deny access to certain users for the purpose of system security. Thus, when you are using ISAM applications, you need to use other protective mechanisms. For example, for access to sensitive data, you can ensure that your access method will be the only one available to unauthorized users.

To accomplish this, you can protect the files that comprise the application data. This can be done by assigning file ownership to a pseudo user or by assigning the files to a group to which no real user belongs. Access permissions then take care that users without privileges will not be allowed access to the data.

If you have thus armed the files against unauthorized access, allow access to users of the program with the assistance of an s-bit program. This program checks whether the user is actually who he says he is, and it checks whether the user has sufficient access rights to perform the requested actions on the data files.

If you need the capability to allow updates to the files by more than one user at the same time, you should implement the ISAM application as a daemon. A service program can receive the database requests from non-privileged users and pass them on to the daemon program, which does the actual reading or writing to the file.

4.2.18   SQL programs

Relational databases use the language SQL (for Structured Query Language). On UNIX systems, SQL programs are implemented using ISAM, so SQL programs cause the same security problems as ISAM applications. In addition, there are some security issues that are only present with SQL programs.

SQL programs store information in files that are accessible to all users. However, you can limit the access by utilizing a privileged program.

A user who has created a table using SQL is automatically the owner of the table. The owner can allow or deny access to other users. This assigned access is valid for an entire table, because every table consists of a file.

For some users, you will want to be able to assign access rights only to certain subsets or columns of data. To do that, you would have to split the database into several tables, but that damages the effectiveness of the database.

Using indirect requests, a user might be able to get information that should not be accessible or should not be for that user. To reach the protected data, it is sufficient to make requests for related data that is not protected. From the resulting combination of such unprotected data, one might be able to draw conclusions about the protected data. This security problem occurs in all database systems.

To make this more difficult, you can minimize the possible range of data requests or introduce random limits on the amount of information that can be extracted with one database request. Unfortunately, both of these methods impede the usability of database systems.

4.3 Programming X Window user interfaces

X clients can temporarily reserve an X display for themselves, using the Xlib call *XGrabServer()*. Only the X client that gets the 'Server Grab' can communicate with the display. During this time, other clients cannot initiate any communication with the display, and connections that had already been started are blocked. Using the Xlib system call *XGrabServer()* can therefore establish a temporary protective barrier for security-specific inputs.

The Xlib call *XOpenDisplay()* will look for the file *.Xauthority* in the home directory of the user. If it exists, it will be opened so that the key for the display can be found. If the key is there, it will be sent to the X server using the X protocol. The X server checks whether the key it receives matches its own key. If they do not match, the X client is refused access and will get an error message.

The Xlib call *XGrabKeyboard*() reserves all keyboard input for the calling X client, so that other X clients will not be able to get at the input. For this reason, however, *XGrabKeyboard*() can only remain active for a limited amount of time in order to keep sensitive input data, such as a password, confidential.

Chapter 5
Planning security management

5.1 Structure of a security
management plan

5.2 Security extensions of UNIX

Managing data security means developing a security plan as well as the adoption and further development of security precautions.

The following sections principally address managers in companies, government agencies, and institutions. They show schematically how to realize data security in an organization.

The plan presented here is a proposal. As the individual responsible for security, you should develop your own data security project tailored to the needs and features of your organization. Of course, there is no simple universal design for planning the management of data security. The normal operations of your organization must be taken into consideration in the planning of the security project in order to ensure its success.

Every organization has a unique operational style and structure; this handbook can only give you general guidelines. Reading this chapter should prepare you to begin planning for a higher level of security. If data security is crucial or your organization's structure, computer systems or applications are very complex, you should consider utilizing external data security consultants or software tools (for example CRAMM, DDIS, MARION, RISKPAC, SBA, SIVOR) to support your planning effort.

5.1 Structure of a security management plan

While creating a security scheme, the individuals and departments involved must realize the meaning of data security for your organization: the threats to data security and what measures are to be used to achieve a more secure system.

Only with appropriate planning can you ensure that the effort to increase data security concentrates on the real security needs of your organization, ignoring speculation, personal preferences or unreal suspicions.

You must develop a security plan especially carefully if your UNIX systems are networked. Networked systems expand the communication capabilities and thus also expand the opportunities for abuse by malicious users.

5.1.1   The data security project

A data security project must be initiated by the office in your organization that is responsible for data processing projects. As with all projects, at the beginning the following are established:

- the project goals
- the project team
- the project expense
- the time constraints on the project.

The data security project can use the same detailed project planning model as is generally used for data processing projects in your organization.

The goal of the project is to develop a catalogue of security measures that increase the data security. The leader of the security team should have experience of software projects and generally should be in a position in the organization that has authority over all the participating departments.

Usually a 'matrix organization' should be considered, which means that the members of the security team continue reporting to their individual group leaders and are only 'loaned out' to the security project leader.

The 'data security' project will certainly meet opposition from the groups involved because, as a rule, increased security is associated with a decrease in system usability. UNIX systems especially make it easy for the user to exchange information with another user on the same machine as well as with a user on a remote UNIX system and even with users on machines running a completely different operating system. Security measures will force restrictions on this comfortable communication. The security team leader's main task is to convince. If the users involved are not convinced of the importance of the security measures, they will try to avoid them.

Depending on the extent of your data security project, it could be useful to work out a formal description of the position which the security project team leader receives at the outset. Such a position description expressly states:

- the tasks to be accomplished by the security team leader;
- who will direct the security team leader, either technically or from a management perspective;

- who will report directly to the security project team leader and what technical or management authority the team leader will have over them;
- who will represent the security team leader in his or her absence.

5.1.2   Establishing the project framework

The project team determines the framework of the project. This means that the project team has to set the limits of the desired data security level, distinguishing from security issues that should not be taken into consideration.

Limitation criteria could be established by:

- limitation to the area 'information processing';
- the division or work site that the security measures should affect;
- financial considerations;
- the given time frame;
- the personnel resources available for the security measures.

5.1.3   Analysis and evaluation of the security risks

When the extent of the work is defined, the project team needs to consider the threats to data security. The project team creates a list of possible threats and the objects that are at risk. 'Objects' are information, data, machines, people and processes that are valuable to the organization.

To analyse the security threats, you can use the so-called 'Delphi method', in which several experts are consulted independently. For the analysis of security threats, the experts should be chosen from a variety of groups. At the beginning of the interview, each expert should be asked to produce a list of three to five threats to data security that occur most often in the everyday operations of your organization. In this way, a list of threats can be collected, from which any meaningless statements and repetitions can be removed.

Thus, a list of real threats is compiled. This list can be used as the foundation for a questionnaire in which each expert is asked to rank the threats according to their probability and importance, using, for example, a scale of one to five. The results of the questionnaires are summarized and distributed to the experts along with another copy of the questionnaire, this time with the request that the threats be ranked again, taking into consideration the previous answers of the other experts. The final results are reached when the experts are in agreement, or when the answers to both questionnaires are unchanged.

To support this method or as an alternative to it, you can use expert systems to perform risk analysis. Risk analysis expert systems perform the function of a human expert, in that they ask the user several questions. The answers are analysed by the expert system, and from the analysis it can create a list of the possible threats to data security and the security precautions needed.

There are different areas of data security that you must analyse. The following should not be taken as a systematic checklist, but instead as a list of examples that are not necessarily complete:

- *Organizational issues*   What tasks or authority does the person responsible for security have? What transfer process is available, what conventions for user logins and files, what programming guidelines? How are employees trained and qualified in security issues? Will requirements for data protection be met?

- *Physical security*   Physical security concerns protection from fire and water damage, as well as from electricity disruptions and surges. Physical security also includes, among other things, access to machines, terminals and communication facilities, which can physically be broken into or damaged.

- *Security of the data*   Is the user or the software developer responsible for data security? Are there mechanisms for confidentiality and logical access protection? How is processed data checked for consistency? What is the data backup methodology?

- *Program security*   Are there programming standards? Is external application software used? How are programs maintained? How is the integrity of the applications guaranteed? How are programs documented?

- *Security of data communication*   This area deals with security issues that relate to remote processing and data transfer. How is identification and authentification of users performed? Does a recipient receive messages unchanged? Are attempts at interception, manipulations, and missent messages reliably prevented?

When you are deciding on the possible threats to consider, ask what basic features of the data systems could be endangered in your case:

- Confidentiality
- Availability
- Integrity

Confidentiality of information and data is maintained when only authorized persons have access to the information and data. Confidentiality is threatened if data can be spied on.

The **availability** of a system is its capability to provide certain services in a reliable form and quality in a reliable amount of time. This includes the availability of information, which means that, in a reliable amount of time, information can be made available in an expected form and quality.

Table 5.1 Weighting scale of threats.

Break-in probability	Amount of damage	Numeric weighting
Very little	Very little	0
Some	Some	1
Medium	Medium	2
Great	Great	4
Very great	Very great	16

Threats to availability include destruction of data by hardware or software errors or sabotage, errors in usage or maintenance, natural disasters (fire, flood, lightning), interruption of electricity or a denial of service because of unauthorized use of system resources. A denial of service results when an illegal user overloads a local area network (LAN) so much that authorized users can no longer use the system.

Integrity is the attribute of a system which only allows intended alterations of information in the system. Information has integrity if only authorized actions affect it and if hardware, information and data are in order.

For each type of security threat and every object at risk, the project team – together with the members of the departments or groups involved – weighs up:

- the probability of a break-in for a given time period, usually the life cycle of a system;
- the amount of damage that could be done. The type of damage could be directly financial or idealistic or a combination of both.

This qualitative weighting is assigned a numeric value. Table 5.1 shows an example of a possible weighting scale.

If all probability p and amount of damage d are weighted numerically for all possible manipulations, you can calculate the potential damage:

```
potentialdamage = p * d
```

This method can be used to create a 'hit list' of potential damage values. You can use the list to separate the serious threats from petty ones. Further work should be limited to the threats associated with the greatest potential damage.

For example, you choose the threats which you have determined to be the twenty highest in terms of potential damage. To decide the number of threats you will deal with, you must consider the amount of effort you will be able to use for security countermeasures.

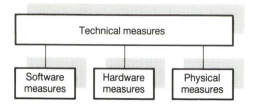

Figure 5.1   Technical measures for increasing data security.

5.1.4   Planning countermeasures

In making the decision whether (and how intensively) a threat should be combated with countermeasures, you can use the following rule of thumb: **The effort required for countermeasures should be at most as great as the value that is at risk from the security threat.**

For objects with the highest potential damage, define **protection levels** corresponding to values you want to protect, for example:

S1 (*weak*)   Protection from unintended violations of data security. Usually, these are user errors.

S2 (*medium*)   Protection from intended violations of security requirements. The protection can be circumvented with medium effort.

S3 (*strong*)   Strong protection that can be overcome only with great effort. Protective measures must be designed so that errors are improbable and easily recognizable.

S4 (*very strong*)   Very strong protection that can be overcome only with extreme effort. Errors are monitored by the UNIX system and are answered with countermeasures.

S5 (*insurmountable*)   Protection that is currently insurmountable. Measures of this protection level are insurmountable for the current state of technology.

At the end of this step, you should have a table that shows to which protection level each object is assigned.

Now the threats and protection requirements for the objects are known. The next step for the project team is to develop various solutions to the security problems that were analysed. Part of this process is deciding what measures are conceivable so that you can make decisions about which should be implemented.

Systematically, you can distinguish between technical and organizational measures. The range of technical measures is shown in Figure 5.1. The measures can then be systematically categorized by the objects to which they correspond.

Figure 5.2 shows the software security measures. This book is designed to give you thorough information about the software measures for the UNIX operating system. UNIX can be utilized to develop measures that protect your applications and data, such as customized access permissions.

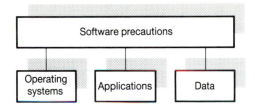

Figure 5.2 Software measures.

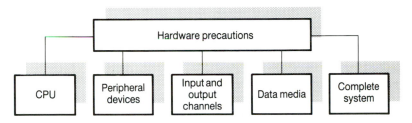

Figure 5.3 Hardware measures.

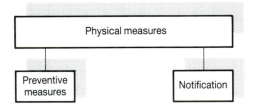

Figure 5.4 Physical measures.

The hardware measures can be organized as shown in Figure 5.3. The CPU and floppy and tape drives can be protected from unauthorized access with mechanical locks. Data storage media can be stored in a locked safe.

Physical measures affect the placement of hardware. Then you can decide whether you will take preventative measures (such as door locks for the hardware room) or have a notification system (an alarm), as shown in Figure 5.4. Physical security also includes building measures to prevent damage from natural disasters (fire, flood, lightning).

Organizational measures can be grouped as shown in Figure 5.5. For example, in the case of personnel security, it should be decided who can be trusted and who is less trustworthy, who is assigned which privileges and responsibilities in the usage of the information system, and so on. A more detailed subdivision of organizational measures distinguishes whether a security measure's structure or flow is affected. Ultimately, it must be decided whether a measure discovers, prevents or alleviates a security threat.

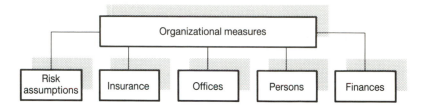

Figure 5.5

The classification of measures described above can serve as a guide for finding security measures. The project team should create a catalogue of measures for each threat being considered, as shown in Table 5.2.

Depending on the number of necessary protection levels, use one or more such forms to list the security measures. Individual measures can complement one another or be used as alternatives to one another. The last step of the planning and decision-making phase consists of choosing which measures should actually be carried out. The same basic criteria should apply as for the classification of objects into different protection levels. You can also orient yourself with a list of additional criteria:

- cost/use relationship;
- independence of the security measure from the 'goodwill' of those involved;
- access permissions only in necessary cases;
- reciprocity of controls, so that no one person is monitoring himself;

Table 5.2   Example of a catalogue of countermeasures.

Threat: System access by unauthorized users
Necessary protection level for threatened objects: S1 (PC), S4 (customer file, salary lists), S5 (results of research)
Catalogue of measures

Type of measure	Level 1	Level 4	Level 5
Physical	No measures	Lock the machine room	Security room for computers and printers
Hardware	No measures	Capability to lock computer	Chipcard system
Software	Password protection	Security auditing system	Chipcard system
Organizational	Security training	Choice of personnel	Monitoring of personnel

- building block principle, so that if a security measure fails, other measures form a security reserve – individual measures should therefore not be independent of each other;
- acceptability.

5.2   Security extensions of UNIX

If the security of UNIX is not sufficient to satisfy the requirements of your organization, there are additional products for making UNIX more secure. Moreover, you can employ one of the UNIX versions for which the architecture was redesigned, so that it complies with government security criteria. Adopted in the USA and European Union, these criteria measure the security of computer systems so that they can be government certified. The following subsections introduce the American and European security criteria and give an overview of the extensions and alternatives to standard UNIX that increase system security.

5.2.1   Choosing secure systems

You can consult government criteria to become familiar with the security extensions or alternatives to the standard UNIX system that could apply to an organization's security requirements. The security criteria include basic information concerning what security functionality is effective against which security threats. Given the security criteria, you can choose the security functionality that corresponds to your security requirements. Product evaluations can give you information about the market for systems that are well suited to your needs. The two most important security criteria are introduced below.

The US security criteria TCSEC

The problem of security in the operation of computer systems was first recognized in the military. In the USA, the Department of Defense published a study in 1983 that defined the general requirements for the security of information in computer systems: *Department of Defense Trusted Computer System Evaluation Criteria*, abbreviated TCSEC. The colour of the cover led to its being commonly referred to as the 'Orange Book'.

The criteria of the Orange Book categorize evaluated computer systems in four groups with the levels A, B, C and D. The groups form a hierarchy of security requirements. Group A includes the highest security requirements, D the lowest. In groups B and C, there is a further subdivision into classes that are also ordered hierarchically. Each security level encompasses the security requirements of the level below it.

The classes are defined as follows:

D: Minimal protection
This class encompasses all systems that do not have software security mechanisms.

C1: Discretionary security protection
C1 requires that the users be able to set and change the accessibility of their objects. In addition, the system requires that users identify themselves as authorized by entering a user name and password.

C2: Controlled access protection
C2 requires more access protection than systems certified as C1. Users of C2 systems can be made responsible for their actions. For this purpose, C2 systems have a login procedure, a security audit system, and protection of the system computing base.

B1: Labelled security protection
B1 contains the protection of mandatory access control (MAC) which dictates which users are allowed to access which objects. For this purpose, users and objects are given security identification called 'labels'. The labels for objects contain a security level such as 'confidential', 'extremely confidential', 'secret', 'top secret'. The labels for users ('subjects') have a category indicating the user's authority.

B2: Structured protection
In addition to MAC, B2 requires a formal system security model. It must be proven that indirect unauthorized information transfer is not possible.

B3: Security domains
B3 requires the isolation of secure areas of the system using hardware. All object access is monitored and recorded by a 'reference monitor'. A trusted path ensures that a user is communicating with the system directly through the terminal. This prevents a spoofing program from reading the user's password input and forwarding it to a potential intruder.

A1: Verified design
For systems qualified A1, a formal mathematical proof is necessary that proves the theoretical correctness of the security module on which the system architecture is based. Another requirement is that it can be shown that no unauthorized transmission of information (covert channel) can occur.

The European security criteria ITSEC

The European Union publishes security criteria for software and systems that supersede the national British, French, Dutch and German security criteria. The European security criteria are called 'Information Technology Security Evaluation Criteria'. They evaluate the security of products and systems (referred

Table 5.3 ITSEC and Orange Book criteria.

ITSEC	Orange Book
E0	D
F-C1, E1	C1
F-C2, E2	C2
F-B1, E3	B1
F-B2, E4	B2
F-B3, E6	B3
F-B3, E6	A1

to as 'Target of Evaluation' or TOE) using two criteria catalogues. One evaluates the accuracy of the implementation, the other the effectiveness of the security functionality. The classifications for accuracy organize the TOE into one eight classes, of which E0 refers to the lowest and E7 to the highest class. The functionality classifications F-C1 through F-B3 are derived from the Orange Book and correspond to the security functionality of the levels C1 through A1. Table 5.3 shows the corresponding classes of the Orange Book and ITSEC.

5.2.2   Audit systems

You can extend UNIX with a program package, so that user actions relevant to security are detected and recorded. This audit record contains information concerning:

- the user who executed the action
- date and time of the action
- the success of the action
- name, type, device, index entry and file system of the objects involved.

Furthermore this 'audit trail' uncovers security violations, so that you can prevent them with suitable measures. If you did not discover the security violation when it occurred, you can use the audit trail to determine the extent of the security problem and apply appropriate countermeasures.

Usually, security violations cannot be recognized by single actions, but by patterns of activity. For example, a user's single refused login attempt could mean that a typing error was made when the password was entered. Many failed login attempts could indicate that an intruder is trying to guess a password. In order to recognize such patterns, you will often need to record numerous events that are part of normal system activity.

Audit packages are event-based systems. They write out data when an event occurs that needs to be recorded. An 'event' is an action that could compromise system security. Events are caused either by system calls or by certain commands (trusted applications) entered by the user. When a system call event occurs, the UNIX system kernel writes the record data in the format of a record of the audit trail.

5.2.3   Access control with smart cards

Cryptographic techniques based on the use of chipcards or 'smart cards' can replace access control using passwords. A smart card is a plastic card that contains a microprocessor (chip). A smart card system may be as follows.

A personal identification number (PIN) that identifies the person in possession of the smart card as the authorized smart card owner is stored in the chip. To log in to the system with the smart card, the user inserts the smart card into the smart card terminal and enters the PIN. The number entered is compared with the PIN that is stored on the smart card.

The smart card and the 'security module' of the computer may have identical secret keys for decrypting messages. The security module sends a randomly generated number to the smart card. In the smart card and in the security module the random number is encrypted into the same key. The results of the two encryptions are compared in the security module. If the results are identical, access is permitted; if they differ, access is denied.

Since the smart card will only generate and encrypt the random number after the PIN is given, the smart card system forces double identification checks. Every identity check is secure from interception and abuse. The PIN and the key cannot be extracted and are stored only in the smart card. Moreover, the user may be able to change the PIN at any time.

5.2.4   C2-secure UNIX

Compared to UNIX systems without security extensions, C2-rated UNIX systems have a more secure access protection using passwords: a password generator ensures that better passwords are chosen and password ageing is mandatory. Furthermore, the encrypted password is not stored in *etc/passwd*. Subjects receive only the privileges that are necessary to execute a defined task. The privileges are in effect only for the execution time. The superuser has fewer rights than in regular UNIX. Service programs relevant to security are stored in the Trusted Computing Base, a specially protected system area. Utilizing access lists (Access Control Lists or ACLs), the user can determine which other users may have access to his or her data.

C2-secure UNIX also has a security record-keeping functionality. It allows monitoring and recording of all user actions relevant to security. For every action, a record is made of the data relating to the action: the time it occurred, which user and terminal number were associated with it and whether the action was successful.

5.2.5   Distributed Computing Environment

Distributed Computing Environment (DCE) is a software package that works with application programs running in a heterogenous networked environment distributed on many machines. DCE supplies machine services that are required by a distributed application program. This makes a number of different machines, operating systems, and networks work together as if based on one single system. The following figure shows the relationship between DCE, operating systems, communications software for networks and application programs.

The DCE security services provide secure communication and controlled access to the databases of the distributed system. There are three main tasks for the security of DCE:

- authentication
- secure communication
- access permissions.

These goals are met by the components of the DCE security services:

- Authentication service
- Privilege service
- Registration service
- Access Control List facility
- Login facility

The authentification service makes it possible for two processes running on different machines to identify themselves to each other. The authentication service is based on the 'Kerberos' network authentification service of the Massachusetts Institute of Technology (MIT). Kerberos works with encryption. The authentication information that is sent over the computer network is encrypted, so that only the intended recipient can decrypt and read the information. Unauthorized users cannot manipulate the encrypted information to break in to the system.

The privilege service determines whether a user should have rights to access a desired object (for example, data). In a secure manner, the privilege service supplies information needed by the server to make decisions about a user's access permissions.

The registration service administers the security database. It contains entries for items relevant to security, called 'principals'. A principal can be a user or a server, for example. The database also contains information for every principal, such as the encryption key. This information is used for authentication, for granting permissions and for the encryption of messages. The system administrator must use the registration service to access and change the database of DCE users.

DCE access lists are lists of users who are allowed to access certain data objects. A user can, for example, enter a colleague into the access list for a file,

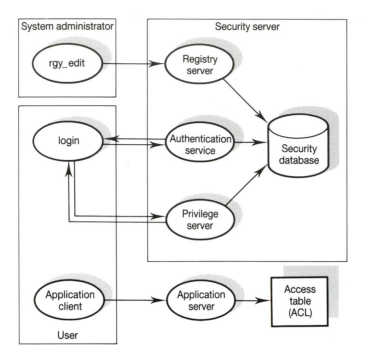

Figure 5.6   DCE security components.

in order to give that person read and write access permission for the file.

The DCE login facility initializes the user's DCE security environment. It authenticates the user by checking the password entered by the user with the security services. The security services reply with a security confirmation, which authorizes the user to whichever distributed services the user accesses during a login session.

Figure 5.6 shows how the security services and functionality of DCE work together to establish security in a distributed environment.

5.2.6   B2 security for UNIX

There are versions of UNIX that are certified at level B2 of the Orange Book. They are distinguished from regular UNIX by the following features:

- privilege mechanism (least privilege mode)
- trustworthy database (trusted computing base)
- user defined access control (discretionary access control)
- system defined access control (mandatory access control)
- security record functionality (audit)

- trustworthy transmission path (trusted path)
- trustworthy system administration (trusted facility management).

The trusted computing base includes all parts of the system that are relevant to security. It consists of the system kernel, programs that have privileged capabilities, libraries used by trusted programs, files that define access permissions for users and the system administrator, system initialization files, security audit record files, and the device files. The trusted computing base is part of a security strategy that protects users from one another, while at the same time protecting the trusted computing base from the users.

Mandatory access control assigns a security level to every user process and object. A security level consists of a hierarchical security class and non-hierarchical optional 'categories'. Security classes could be, for example, 'confidential', 'extremely confidential', 'secret' and 'top secret'. A category is ordered by subject area. An organization could have categories such as 'product planning', 'development' and 'management'. A security level has the format:

```
Security_class: Category1, Category2, ...
Categories
```

The name of a security level could look like this:

```
Confidential: development, management
```

The system compares the user's security level with that of the object the user wants to access. The access will be allowed if the user's security level is equal to or higher than the security level of the object.

Discretionary access control (DAC) works using access tables (Access Control Lists, or ACLs), giving the user the capability to allow individual users access to files. All users not entered in the ACL for a particular file are denied access to it. The ACLs extend the access mechanism of basic UNIX. Every file has an ACL.

The trusted facility management of B2-rated UNIX divides the privileges of the UNIX superusers among five different partial sets of privileges, reserved for various system administration 'roles':

- Security administrator, who assigns security levels to system objects;
- Security auditor, who administers the monitoring system;
- Operator, who performs non-privileged routine system administration;
- Security operator, who performs privileged routine system administration;
- Network administrator.

Chapter 6
Important commands and system calls

6.1   Commands   6.2   System calls

This chapter provides descriptions of commands and system calls that deal with UNIX system security. The commands in this chapter are important either because they need to be used with caution to avoid endangering system security, or because they serve as tools for the monitoring of user activity.

The description of commands and system calls in this chapter concentrates on information that is important to system security. You can find additional information in your UNIX manuals.

6.1   Commands

UNIX commands can become a security risk if they are used in a way that makes it easier for a malicious user to do damage. Several commands make it easier for you to have a good overview and control of the other users of the system. You can gain a thorough overview of user activity by using a security auditing system, which can be installed as an extension of your UNIX system.

at – Execute commands at a later time

The command *at*:

- reads commands from a file and executes them at a later time:

  at[¬-**f**¬file] [¬-**q**queue] ¬time[¬date] [¬+increment]

- prints to the standard output the *at* command jobs that have not yet been processed:

  at¬-**l**[¬job_number]

- deletes from the queue jobs started by *at* or *batch*:

  at ¬-**r**¬job_number¬...

---

at[¬-**f**¬file] [¬-**q**queue] ¬time[¬date] [¬+increment]
at¬-**l**[¬job_number]
at ¬-**r**¬job_number¬...

The file */var/spool/cron/atjobs* especially needs protection:

> This is the directory containing the *at*-jobs that have not yet been execut-
> ed. For each *at*-job there is a corresponding file named *job_number.a*.
> These files have the permissions -r--S--S--- . If a malicious user can alter
> these files, the jobs could execute something other than what the user
> intended.
> For this reason pay particular attention to ensuring that other users do not
> get write permissions for the directory where the jobs are stored.

You should also protect the file */etc/cron.d/at.allow* from unauthorized access.
This file contains a list of user login accounts with execution permissions for *at*.

You can enter in the file */etc/cron.d/at.deny* the user logins that should be
denied execution permissions for *at*. Only the owner should have read and write
permissions for this file.

cd – Change working directory

The command *cd*, which is built into the Bourne shell *sh*, makes the given directory your current directory.

In a restricted shell the command *cd* is not allowed.

```
cd[¬directory]
```

You have to have execute permission for *directory*. If you give the *directory* as a relative or absolute pathname, you will need to have execute rights for all the directories in the path.

In the Bourne shell, the given directory will be found without the environment variable *CDPATH*, if the name begins with one of the following characters:

> /   indicates that the search will start at / (root).
> ./   indicates that the search will begin at the current directory.
> ../ indicates that the search will begin in the directory above the current directory.

If the name of the given directory does not begin with any of these characters, *cd* will evaluate the environment variable *CDPATH* as follows:

- If *CDPATH* is not defined or is empty, *cd* will look for the given directory relative to the current working directory.
- If *CDPATH* is assigned a value, *cd* will search the paths in the *CDPATH* value for the given path. If a directory is found, it will write out to the standard output the absolute pathname of the directory.

If *directory* is not given:

> The command *cd* with no argument changes the current directory to be your HOME directory. The HOME directory is identical to your login directory, unless you have set your shell variable HOME to a different directory name.

chgrp – Change the group ID of a file

chgrp sets a new group for a file or a directory.

---

chgrp¬[**-R**]¬[**-h**]¬newgroup¬file¬...

-R

> Recursively changes all the given directories and all directories under the given directories. *chgrp* also follows symbolic links.

-h

> If *file* is a symbolic link, *chgrp* will change its group ID. Without the option, it will change the group ID of the file pointed to by the symbolic link.

newgroup

> New group name or group ID number. *newgroup* must already be entered in the file */etc/group*.

file

> Name of the file that will get the new group ID. *file* can also be a directory. More than one name can be given.

Security

Only the system administrator is allowed to change the group for an arbitrary file. With the operating system option *_POSIX_CHOWN_RESTRICTED*, ordinary users' ability to change groups can be restricted. If this option is set, users will only be able to change the group of their own files. The user then must:

- be entered in the file */etc/group* as a member of the new group given in the *chgrp* call.

- currently belong to this new group. In other words, the user must change his or her current group using the command *newgrp* before the call to *chgrp*.

If *chgrp* is used by a user who has no system administrator privileges, all s-bits set for the given files will be cleared (set-user-ID and set-group-ID, see *chmod*).

crypt – Encode and decode text

crypt encodes and decodes the contents of files. It reads from the standard input and writes to the standard output.

Files that are encrypted without using the option *-c* are compatible with files that have been created or changed using in encrypt mode of the editors *ed*, *edit*, *ex* or *vi*.

---

crypt [¬-c] [¬key]	Format 1
crypt [¬-k]	Fuimat 2

The data security of encrypted files depends primarily on the following conditions:

- The encrypting mechanism used cannot be recognized.
- The encryption password key should not be accessible with any direct search.
- 'Hidden doors', where the encryption or even the original text is recognizable, should be as rare as possible.

If you concatenate two or more files, encrypted using the same key, into one file and later try to decode this file, only the contents of the first of the concatenated files will be decrypted correctly.

When you give your encryption key as argument to command *crypt*, other users could find out the key by executing *ps* or other similar commands. The primary weaknesses of *crypt* are the choice of the password key and the encoding security.

If you pipe the output into *nroff* but don't include the password key in the command, you won't be allowed to connect *crypt* with the command *pg* since commands like *pg* change the terminal output settings.

cu – Call UNIX – connect to another UNIX system

cu establishes a connection to another UNIX system, to a workstation or to another machine with another operating system. *cu* executes in two phases. In the first, the connection phase, the connection is established. In the second, the communication phase, data are transferred to and from the remote system.

```
cu[¬-sbaudrate][¬-ctyp][¬-lline][¬-b{7|8}]
[¬-dehnot][¬target]¬
```

The file */etc/uucp/Devices* has a list of media that are available on your system. The file */etc/uucp/Systems* contains information needed for connection with remote systems; for security reasons, this file should not be publicly readable.

Files

/etc/uucp/Sysfiles
/etc/uucp/Systems
/etc/uucp/Devices
/var/spool/locks/*

find – Search directories

find searches in directories for files, directories or FIFO, that satisfy conditions given by the user.

---

find¬directory¬...¬expression

You can use *find* to search for files, directories, and device files that allow write permission for 'others' and therefore constitute a security risk.

To search for files, directories, and device files that give 'others' write permission, use the following *find* command:

```
$ find / -perm -2 ! \( -type l -o -type p -o
-type s \) -print
```

The write permission for 'group' can be just as big a security risk as write permission for 'others'. If all users on the system belong to the group *user*, then write permission for the group *user* is the same as write permission for 'others'. To search for files that are writable for the group *user*, use the following *find* command:

```
$ find / -perm -020 -group user !\( -type l -o
-type p -o -type s \) -print
```

You can check whether initialization files such as *.profile* or *.ksh* have write permissions for 'group' and 'others', thus constituting a security risk. Use *find* to look for filenames that begin with a dot:

```
$ find / -perm -2 -o -perm -20 -name .\* -print
```

Look for files with the s-bit set, using

```
$ find / \( -perm -002000 -o -perm -004000 \) -print
```

To search for shell procedures that use the s-bit, use the following command line:

```
$ find / \( -perm -002000 -o -perm -004000 \)\
-exec /bin/file {} \; | grep "commands text"
```

ftp – File transfer program

The command *ftp* performs transmission of data between machines in a network.

---

ftp[¬**-dgintv**][remote_machine]

Options relevant to system security:

-d

> (d - debug) turns on test help mode. *ftp* prints to the screen every command that will be sent to the remote machine (see also *ftp* command *debug*).
>
> If you log in to the remote machine using the command *user*, the machine will prompt for your password. If you have called *ftp* with the option *-d*, when you enter your password, it will be shown on the screen.

-n

> (n – no auto-login) disables the automatic prompting for user login and password when establishing the connection. In this case, use the *ftp* command *user* for logging in to the remote system.
>
> no *-n* given:
>
> *ftp* will search the file *.netrc* in the home directory on the local machine. This file can include entries for user logins from the remote machine. If there is no such entry or the file *.netrc* does not exist, *ftp* will require that you log in using a user name and password. If you have the same user name on the remote machine as on the local machine, then at the prompt for user name you only need to press XXX followed by your password.

For information on the contents and format of the file *.netrc* see below.

The file .netrc

As soon as you have called *ftp* or the *ftp* command *open* together with the name of the remote machine, the file *.netrc* is found and processed. It contains data for the login on the remote machine for *ftp* data transmission. The file must be provided in the HOME directory on the local machine and should have the access permissions *-rw-------* , because it contains passwords.

The login data is specified using keywords and their values. All keywords can be defined more than once. The keyword and its value must be separated from each other and from the next keyword by blanks, tabs, or new line characters. The following keywords are available:

machine¬remote_machine

gives the machine to or from which you want to be able to transfer files. If *remote_machine* matches the machine name given in the *ftp* call or in the command *open*, then the rest of the keywords will be processed.

login¬user_login

the user login name on the remote machine.

password¬password

gives the password for *user_login*.

If this keyword exists and if the file *.netrc* is readable for 'others', *ftp* will halt the auto-login process.

account¬password2

gives an additional password.

macdef¬macro-name

defines a macro. If you name the macro *init*, then *macdef* will be the last keyword processed.

Anonymous ftp

ftp can be configured for 'anonymous' access, so that files can be left or retrieved by users who do not have logins on your system. If you want to use anonymous *ftp* you enter *anonymous* for the user login name. On many systems you can also log in as *ftp*. For the password you usually use your first or last name.

To make anonymous *ftp* available for other users, you must create a user login *ftp*. The files that are sent or received by *ftp* will be stored in the user *ftp*'s HOME directory. You should isolate the login *ftp* from other user logins in a special directory, for example as */usr/spool/ftp*. To give users a place where they are allowed to leave files on your system anonymously, you could create a directory *~ftp/pub* or *~ftp/pub/anonym*, and set the access permissions on the directory to *1777*. This will give all users read, write, and execute permissions to the directory.

Security

If you want to transfer files using *ftp*, you must log in to the remote system by giving a user account and password. The login is logged in the file */usr/adm/wtmp*. Because the password is transmitted over the network, it could be intercepted. Thus, for security on some systems, the *ftp* program should be disabled.

Restrictions on ftp

The file */etc/inet/ftpusers* contains a list of users who are **not** allowed to transfer files using *ftp*.

/etc/inet/ftpusers should include all system user accounts such as *root*, *uucp*, *bin*, or *daemon*.

kill – Send signals to processes

The *kill* command sends a signal to a set of processes, given by process number.

`kill[¬-signal]¬process_number¬...`	Format 1
`kill¬-signal¬-group_number¬...`	Format 2
`kill¬-1`	Format 3

You can use the command *kill* to terminate the processes of a user who has gained unauthorized access to the system. The command *ps* can give you a listing of the process numbers of the unauthorized user's processes. Using *passwd*, change the password of the user login in which the break-in occurred.

Change the password first before terminating the processes, especially when the intruder is logged in to the system as *root*. If you don't follow this order, the intruder could use the superuser privileges to throw you off the system.

kill sends a signal to the process that is to be interrupted or terminated. Below is a description of the signals that are important for UNIX users.

In contrast to the signals that can be caught by programs (for example SIGTERM), the signals SIGKILL (Signal 9) and SIGSTOP (Signal 17) cannot be caught by programs.

Format 1: Send signals to processes

`kill[¬-signal]¬processnumber¬...`

-signal

Signal to be sent to the process. The following signals are meaningful at the command level:

Signal number	Symbolic name	Meaning
1	SIGHUP	connection to the monitor is interrupted (hangup)
2	SIGINT	interrupt with XXX
3	SIGQUIT	terminate (quit)
9	SIGKILL	unconditional termination (kill)
15	SIGTERM	software termination

processnumber

Number of the process to which you want to send a signal.

Users who do not have system administrator privileges can only send signals to their own processes. The system administrator can send signals to all processes.

The *ps* command lists the current processes.

The process number 0 means: The given signal will be sent to all processes from your process group.

Format 2: Send signals to process groups

```
kill¬-signal¬-groupnumber¬...
```

-signal

  Signal to be sent to a process group.

-groupnumber

  kill sends the signal to all process of the process group *groupnumber*.

Format 3: List symbolic signal names

kill¬-l

-l

  kill lists the symbolic signal names.

last – List last user or last terminal login

With *last*, you can find out users' login and logout times.

---

last [¬-[**n**¬]number] [¬-**f**¬filename] [¬name]

No argument given
> *last* prints all login and logout times recorded in the file */var/adm/wtmpx* and tells the date of the oldest entry with the message `wtmpx begins with date`.

-[**n**]number
> the number of login and logout times printed out should not exceed *number*.

-**f**¬filename
> Read login and logout times from the file *filename*. Default is the file */var/adm/wtmpx*.

name
> Name of the user and/or a terminal (*term/tty001*). There can be more than one name.

Methodology

Logins and logouts are recorded in the file */var/adm/wtmpx*. *last* gets information about a user and the associated terminal from this file.

The arguments for *last* indicate the user names or terminals to be listed. The complete terminal name must be given.

By default, *last* prints a record of all login and logout times in descending order. If you give it as argument a certain user or terminal, then only the data concerning the given user or terminal will be printed. If you give it several arguments, the information requested with each argument will be printed.

last also notes whether a login session is still ongoing or was terminated by a *reboot*.The pseudo-user *reboot* logs itself in when a reboot is started on the system. Then, the message *last reboot* gives the times between reboots.

ln – *Create a reference to a file (link)*

ln creates a link to a file. With a link, you can access a file through a different name or pathname.

```
ln[¬-f][¬-n][-s¬]file[...]¬target
```

If no option is given

ln creates an ordinary link. If there is a file with the same name that the new link is supposed to have and you don't have write permission for that file, *ln* will print the permissions on the file and ask whether it should create the link.

-f

(f – force) If there is already a file with the name *target*, *ln* will force the link to be created without prompting, whether or not you have write permission for the file.

-n

If there is already a file with the name *target*, *ln* will not overwrite the contents of the file.

The option *-f* overrides the option *-n*.

-s

ln creates a symbolic link to *file*. *file* does not have to exist already. *target* can be a directory.

file

Name of the file to which you want to make a link. The file must exist already. *file* cannot be a directory.

target

Name of the link which you want to create for *file*. For *target*, you can use simply a filename or an absolute or relative pathname.

Ordinary links

When *ln* creates a link to a file, the link is entered as a filename in the directory. The entry gets the same index number as the old file. The same index number is then valid for both filenames and thus the access permissions, owner and data are also identical. The file, referred to by the filename, exists physically only once. You can now refer to one file with several filenames or pathnames.

You can determine with the index number whether two files are linked to the same file (see *ls -i*). The link count tells you how many links there are to the file, that is, how many directory entries exist for that file (see *ls -l*).

You can delete a directory entry with *rm*. If there is more than one link to the file, then the file will remain accessible under the other name(s). Only when the last reference to the file is deleted will *rm* physically remove the file.

Symbolic Links

A symbolic link is a file that contains a pathname. In this way, a pathname is duplicated as another pathname. There is no mechanism for counting symbolic links.

 When a symbolic link is deleted, the file expressed in the pathname is also deleted.
The index entry (i-node) of a file which has a symbolic link to it contains no information that a symbolic link exists. The link count keeps track only of regular links. So, if you delete the target of a symbolic link, the symbolic link will still exist, but it will point to a file that is empty and has no i-node.

 Symbolic links are not bound by file systems.
The pathname can be the name of a file or a directory.
Symbolic links are visible with the ls command:

- To determine which files are symbolic links in a given directory, use the command *ls -l*. You can also read the contents of the symbol links with this command, indicated by the path that follows the arrow, '–>' .

- Using the command *ls -L*, you can get information about the file pointed to by the symbolic link.

Operations that use '..' within symbolically linked directories, such as '*cd ..*', will refer to the original directory!

login – Log in to the system

login takes care of the identification and authentication of users when they log in to the system.

---

login[¬user_login[¬environment...]]

---

user_login

The user login into which you want to initiate a new login session. This user login must be entered in the file */etc/passwd*.

If *user_login* is not given:
The command *login* will prompt for it on the next line.

If the */etc/shadow* file indicates that there is a password for this user login, then *login* will require that you enter the password.

Your input will not be shown on the screen and will not be logged in any file.

environment

Assignment of an environment variable, which can be given in the form *yyy* or *xxx=yyy*. Variables can be assigned on the command line or along with the input of the user login name. *xxx* indicates the name of the environment variable. *yyy* is the value to be assigned to the variable. Using backslash, ' \ ', you can escape individual characters in *yyy*, such as blank and tabulators.

xxx=yyy

The environment variable *xxx* is assigned the value *yyy*. Old values of the environment variable will be overridden by this assignment, with two exceptions: *PATH* and *SHELL* cannot be overridden this way.

yyy

The environment variable *Lnumber* is assigned the value *yyy*. *number* begins at 0 and is incremented for each of the given *yyy* values.

Methodology of the login command

The command *login* compares the given user login and password with the corresponding entry in the */etc/passwd* file. If both are correct, you will be logged in to this user login account.

If the information is not correct, after five failed login attempts the connection to the workstation or terminal is interrupted. This will also happen if you do not enter the requested information within a certain amount of time.

During login, the command *login* executes the following tasks in order:

- *login* looks in */etc/passwd* for the user number (UID) and group number (GID) that correspond to the user login given.

The operating system administers the user logins internally using only the user and group ID numbers.

- *login* enters the user login into the file */etc/utmp*. This file contains the logins of all users who are currently logged in to the system.
  The command *who* accesses this file.

- *login* enters the user login into the file */var/adm/wtmp*. If this log file exists, a record of all logins and logouts are written to it continuously.

- *login* prints out when the last login for this account took place. This information is stored in the file */var/adm/lastlog*.

- */etc/motd* is printed.

- *login* assigns default values to the following environment variables:

Variable	Assignment:
HOME	name of the login directory (from /etc/passwd)
LOGNAME	login user account (from /etc/passwd)
MAIL	/var/mail/user_login
SHELL	/usr/bin/sh (from /etc/passwd)
TZ	MET-1
PATH	/usr/bin
LANG	NLS-variable that defines an internationalized environment
TTY	terminal number
TERM	type of terminal
USER	login user account

- *login* sets the current directory to be the login directory that, in */etc/passwd*, is set in the entry for this user login.

- *login* starts the program that is set in */etc/passwd* for this user login. Ordinarily, */usr/bin/sh* is started as the login shell. This shell is overlaid on the *login* process.

  If the program name in */etc/passwd* is the entry *, then the given login directory will become the root directory: it will look for filenames that begin with slash starting from this directory. *login* will be executed again at the new root structure.

ls – List contents of a directory

Using *ls*, you can list information about files and directories.

`ls`[¬option]...[¬file]...

Options relevant to security:

-a

All files are listed, including those that begin with a dot.

-b

Print non-printable characters in the octal format *ddd*.

-d

If *file* is a directory, *ls* will list its name (not its contents). If *file* is not given, the output of *ls* will include a dot for the current directory.

-f

ls handles every argument as a directory and prints out the directories in the order in which they were listed.

-F

Directories are represented by a slash / following the name. Files that are declared as executable are printed with the suffix ⋆. The at sign @ indicates a symbolic link.

-i

The index number (i-node) of every file and directory is shown in the first column of the output.

-l

With 'long listing', *ls* will give complete information.

Access permissions
Three sets with three characters each show the access permissions:

- of the owner of the file (characters 1 to 3),
- for the members of the group (characters 4 to 6),
- for all other users (characters 7 to 9).

In each set, the character in the

1st position: *r* stands for read permission or – for no read permission
2nd position: *w* for write permission or – for no write permission
3rd position: *x* stands for execute permission
         s for execute permission plus the s-bit set
         t for execute permission plus the t-bit set (sticky-bit)
         T for the t-bit set without execute permisssion

> *S* for the l-bit
> – stands for nothing set, neither execute permission nor
> any special bit

If the s-bit and x-bit (execute permission) are set at the same time for the owner or the group, then there will be an *s* in place of an *x*. The s-bit cannot be set without the corresponding x-bit.

In the x-bit position, there can also be an *S*, if the l-bit is set for the file, that is, if mandatory locking is in effect for this file. In this case neither the x-bit nor the s-bit can be set for the group. The read and write permissions for a file with the l-bit set can be locked by a program that uses the function *lockf()*, as long as this program is accessing the file (see *chmod*).

There can be *t* or *T* in the position of the x-bit for other users. *T* or *t* represents the sticky-bit status (t-bit). *T* stands for set sticky-bit without the x-bit and *t* stands for set sticky-bit with the x-bit set (see *chmod*).

Number of links
Decimal number that gives the number of links to the file, at least 1.

User login of the owner
Login name of the owner of the file.

Group name
Group name of the owner of the file.

Size in bytes
Decimal number that indicates the size of the file in bytes.

If a device file is given, instead of the file size, it shows the major and minor device numbers.

Month, day, time
This gives the date and time of the last change to the file.

Filename
In addition to the size of individual files, if this is a directory it will show the size of the directory in 512-byte blocks. If the file or directory is a symbolic link, then an arrow –> after the filename is followed by the pathname of the file to which it is linked.

You should also be aware that in an environment using remote file sharing, you do not always have the permissions indicated by the output of *ls -l*.

-L

> With symbolic links, this will output the link name for the original file or
> directory.

-n

In the place of the name of the owner or group, this option will print the user or group ID number; otherwise the output is like that of *-l*.

-o

The group is not shown; otherwise same as *-l*.

-p

A slash / after object names indicates that they are directories.

-q

A non-printable character in a filename is printed as a question mark ?.

-R

If *file* is not given, the names of all files and directories in the current directory will be printed, followed by all its subdirectories and their component file and directories.

-s

In addition to filenames, the size of each file is printed in the first column expressed in 512-byte units.

-t

Instead of sorting by filename, sort the files by date of the last change: the file with the most recent date first.

-u

In combination with the option *-t*:
The objects are sorted according to the time of the last access.
In combination with the option *-l*:
Instead of the time of the last change to the file, the time of the last access is printed.

mail – Send or receive messages

With *mail*, you can send and receive mail.

```
mail[¬-tw] [¬-m¬message_type]¬recipient¬...
```
                                                    Format 1
```
mail[¬-ehpPqr] [¬-f¬file]
```
                                                    Format 2
```
mail¬-F¬recipient¬...
```
                                                    Format 3
```
mail¬-T¬mailsurr-file¬recipient¬...
```
                                                    Format 4
```
mail[¬-xdebug-level] [¬other-mail-
options...]¬recipient¬...
```
                                                    Format 5

Format Descriptions

Format 1: Send mode
mail[¬-tw][¬-m¬message_type]¬recipient¬...
-t

> (t – to) *mail* adds a line in the heading of the letter, of the form *To: recipient* for each of the intended recipients.

-w

> (w – wait) *mail* sends a letter to a remote user without waiting for the completion of the remote transfer program.

-m¬message_type

> (m – message type) *mail* will add the line *Message-Type: message_type* to the heading. *message_type* can be any arbitrary text string.

recipient

> is any valid user login name on the local system or a net path, if the machine is connected to a network. You can name more than one recipient.

Format 2: Read mode
mail[¬-ehpPqr][¬-f¬file]
If no options are given

> *mail* will check the default mail box */var/mail/$USER*. If there are messages, *mail* will print the last message received (last in – first out).

-e

> *mail* checks whether there is any mail. If there are messages, *mail* will return with an exit value of 0, otherwise a value of 1 is returned. Then *mail* will terminate.

-h

> (h – header) *mail* shows the contents of the UNIX postmark lines for all mail messages in the order of their arrival, beginning with the most recently received.

-p

(p – print) *mail* prints all messages without prompting in the order of their arrival, beginning with the most recently received. Then, *mail* will terminate.

-P

(P – print) *mail* prints all mail messages individually along with their header lines in the order of their arrival, beginning with the most recently received.

-q

(q – quit) *mail* will terminate at the signal SIGINT (XXX key).

-r

(r – reverse) *mail* will output the messages in first in, first out order.

-f¬mailbox

(f – file) *mail* reads the messages from the file *mailbox*.

Format 3: Forward mode
mail¬-F¬recipient...
-F

(F – forward) *mail* will cause all incoming mail to be forwarded to *recipient*, provided the mailbox is currently empty.

recipient

is a list with a maximum length of 1024 bytes. If more than one user is specified, the whole list should be enclosed in double quotes so that it may all be interpreted as the operand of the -F option. Either commas or white space can be used to separate users.

To terminate forwarding mode, give a NULL argument for the *recipient* (*mail -F ""*).

If there is a pipe symbol before the recipient, the rest of the line will be interpreted as a command and the incoming mail is passed as input to the command.

Format 4 and 5: Debug mode
mail¬-T¬mailsurr-file¬recipient¬...
mail[¬-xdebug-level][¬other-mail-options]...¬recipient¬...
-T¬mailsurr-file

(T – test) This option supports the system administrator's modification of the *mailsurr* file. This file contains commands, called surrogate commands, that are used by *mail* for routing and transport of mail messages.

mailsurr-file is an arbitrary file name. If you use an empty string (*-T ""*), *mail* uses the default file */etc/mail/mailsurr*.

mail reads any message from the standard input and records the processing of the *mailsurr-file* on the standard output without actually sending the mail.

recipient

> Name of the recipient or recipients with whom the *mailsurr-file* is to be tested.

-x

> *mail* creates a file called */tmp/MLDBGprocessnumber*, which contains information about how *mail* processed the current message.
>
> This information is more complete than the information you get using the option *-T* and, for this reason, is especially of interest to the system administrator.

debug_level

> specifies a negative or positive integer. The absolute value of *debug_level* determines the amount of information provided. If *debug_level* is greater than 0, there is no information printed unless *mail* has difficulties with the processing of the message. If *debug_level* is less than 0, a data relevant to the processing will be recorded. If *debug_level* is 0, no debug information will be printed.

other-mail-options

> *mail* send options to be tested.

recipient

> Name of the recipient or recipients for whom the send mechanism is to be tested.

mkdir – Make a directory

Use *mkdir* to create a new directory.

---

mkdir [¬option] ¬directory¬...

If no option is given

> *mkdir* creates a directory with the name *directory* with access permissions 777 (see *chmod*). Using the command *umask*, you can change the defaults for the access permissions (see *umask*).

-m¬mode

> (m – mode) *mkdir* creates the new *directory* with the access permissions given in *mode* (see *chmod*).

-p

> (p – parent) *mkdir* first creates all parent directories given in the pathname *directory* that do not yet exist before the directory is created.

directory

> Name of the directory to be created. You can give more than one directory.

> For *directory*, you can use absolute or relative pathnames.

> The new directory will be assigned the real user and group ID numbers of the calling process.

passwd – Enter or change password and password attributes

passwd enters a new user password or changes an existing one in the file */etc/shadow*.

---

passwd[¬option][¬user_login]

If no option is given

> The password that will be changed is the password of the user login in which you are logged in. If you get into another user account with *su*, *passwd* will produce the error message: *permission denied*.

Options for non-privileged users

-s

> (s – show) The password attributes for the login *name* will be displayed in the following format:
>
> *name status mm/dd/yy minimum maximum warningday*
>
> or, if password ageing information is not present,
>
> *name status*
>
> where
>
> *name*

> The login ID of the user.

status

> The current password status of the user *name*: *PS* stands for passworded or locked; *LK* stands for locked; *NP* stands for no password.

mm/dd/yy

> The date the password was last changed for *name*. This date is expressed in UTC/GMT (Universal Time Coordinate/Greenwich Mean Time) and could therefore be out by up to a day in other time zones.

minimum

> The minimum number of days that must elapse between password changes for *name*. Default is the value of *MINWEEKS* from the file */etc/default/passwd*.

maximum

The maximum number of days a password can be valid for *name*. Default is the value of MAXWEEKS from the file */etc/default/passwd*.

warningday

The number of days before the password expires that the user will be warned.

Options and arguments for system administrators

-l

(l – lock) The password for *user_login* will be locked.

-d

(d – delete) The password for *user_login* will be removed. Then, during login, there will be no prompt for a password.

Warning

If the system administrator deleted a user's password using the option *-d* and time restrictions are in effect for the user, the user will not have to enter a new password. This is also true when the entry *PASSREQ* in the file */etc/login/default* is set to the value *YES*. The user then no longer has a password. **Therefore you should always use the -d option in combination with the -f option**. That way the users are forced to give a password the next time they try to log in.

-n min

Between two password changes at least *min* number of days must elapse. If *min* is greater than *max*, then the user will not be able to change the password. *-n* should always be used in combination with the option *-x*.

-x max

The password for *user_login* will be valid for a maximum of *max* days. If *max* has the value -1, the password time limit will no longer be checked for this *user_login* and the user will be forced to change the password at the next login attempt.

-w warn

The user will be warned *warn* number of days before their password expires.

-a

(a – all) The password attributes of all entries will be listed. Use *-a* only in combination with *-s*. The *user_login* does not have to be given in this case.

-f

(f – force) The password for *user_login* becomes invalid. The password must be changed the next time the user logs in.

user_login

This is the user login to which the new password belongs. This operand only makes sense for use by the system administrator. If you are not the system administrator, you are only allowed to give your own user login.

If *user_login* is not given:

passwd changes the password for the current user login.

passwd enters a new password or changes an existing password in the file */etc/shadow*. In addition, some password attributes can be changed and listed.

Every user can have their password attributes printed out. Users who do not have system administrator permissions can only change their own passwords and the associated attributes. The system administrator can change any user's passwords and attributes on the local system.

If the user does not have system administrator permissions, *passwd* will require the old password if there is one.

Then *passwd* will prompt for a new password. The new password must be entered twice to avoid typing errors. Passwords are not shown on the screen as they are typed in.

When the old password is entered, *passwd* checks whether the expiry conditions are met. If not, *passwd* will terminate. If there were no special expiry conditions (options *-n* and *-x*), the standard values *MAXWEEK* and *MINWEEK* from the file */etc/default/passwd* will be used. If expiry conditions were set, that information in */etc/shadow* will not change.

If the expiry conditions are met, *passwd* will check whether the new password has the correct format.

A password:

- must be at least *PASSLENGTH* characters long. *PASSLENGTH* is set in the file */etc/default/passwd*. *PASSLENGTH* must contain a minimum of six characters. *passwd* evaluates only the first eight characters of the password, even when PASSLENGTH is greater than eight.

- must have at least two alphabetic characters and at least one numeric or special character. The alphabetic characters can be upper case or lower case.

- must differ from the user's login name, and any reverse or circular shift of the login name. When this comparison is made, it does not distinguish between upper-case and lower-case letters.

- must differ from the old passwords by at least three characters. When this comparison is made, it does not distinguish between upper- and lower-case letters.

The system administrator does not need to input the old password and the new password entered is not checked for the correct format. System administrators are not forced to comply with password ageing and password construction requirements. A system administrator can create a null password by entering only XXX in response to the prompt for the new password. In contrast to *passwd -d*, there will be a prompt for a password at login.

ps – Process status

```
ps[¬-adeflcj][¬g¬grplist][¬-p¬proclist]
[¬-t¬termlist][¬-u¬uidlist][¬-s¬sesslist]
```

If no options are given

ps prints information about processes associated with the controlling terminal or workstation. The output consists of a brief listing.

-a

Print information about all processes associated with a terminal, with the exception of process group leaders.

-c

Print information about the control process *scheduler*. *-c* influences the output of the options *-f* and *-l*.

-d

Prints information about all processes with the exception of process group leaders.

-e

Prints information about all processes.

-f

(f – full list) Generates a more complete listing of information about the individual processes including UID, PPID, C, CLS and STIME.

-g¬grplist

List only process data whose process group leader's ID number(s) appears in *grplist*.

-j

List the ID numbers of the session and the process group.

-l

(l – long list) Generates a listing of complete information about the individual processes.

-p¬proclist

List only process data whose process ID numbers are given in *proclist*.

-s¬sesslist

List only information about the process group leaders whose process numbers are given in *sesslist*.

-t¬termlist

List only process data associated with the terminal given in *termlist*.

-u¬uidlist

List only process data whose user ID number or login name is given in *uidlist*.

Output

The column headings and the meaning of the columns in a *ps* listing are given in the following text. The letters in parentheses indicate the option that causes the corresponding heading to appear. *all* means that the heading always appears. Note that these two options (*-f* for *full* and for *long*) determine only what information is provided for a process; they do not determine which processes will be listed.

F (*l*)

> Flags (hexadecimal and additive) associated with the process. The flags and their meanings are machine dependent and therefore are not listed here.

S (*l*)

> The state of the process:
>
> 0   Process is currently running.
>
> S   Sleeping: process is waiting for an event to complete.
>
> R   Ready: process is in the queue.
>
> I   Idle: process is being created
>
> Z   Zombie state: process terminated and parent process not waiting – has not yet called the wait( ) system call
>
> T   Traced: process stopped by a signal from its parent, which is tracing it.
>
> X   SXBRK state: process is waiting for more primary memory.

UID (*f*, *l*)

> (UID – user ID) The user ID number of the process owner. If the option *-f* is used, the login name is printed instead of the UID. Only the first seven characters of the user login name are printed.

PID (*all*)

> (PID – process ID) The process number. Every process is assigned a unique identification number when it is created. This number is needed to terminate a process using *kill*.

PPID (*f*, *l*)

> (PPID – parent process ID) The process ID of the parent process.

C (*f*, *l*)

> Processor utilization for scheduling.

CLS (*c*)

> Scheduling group (processes, which are handled in time slices).

PRI (*l*,*c*)

> The priority of the process. Higher numbers normally mean lower priority. If the option *-c* is given, then the reverse is true: higher numbers mean higher priority.

NI (*l*)

> Nice value, used in priority computation (see *nice*). Only *time-sharing* processes have a nice value.

ADDR (*l*)

> The memory address (physical page frame number) of the user's memory if the process is resident, otherwise the disk address of the swapped out process.

SZ (*l*)

> The size of the core image of the process in blocks.

WCHAN (*l*)

> The address of an event for which the process is waiting. If the column is empty, the process is running.

STIME (*f*)

> The starting time of the process, given in hours, minutes and seconds. A process begun more than 24 hours before the *ps* inquiry is executed is given by date.

TTY (*all*)

> The controlling terminal for the process (the message, ?, is printed when there is no controlling terminal).

TIME (*all*)

> The cumulative execution time for the process, given in minutes and seconds.

COMD (*all*)

> The command name (the full command name and its arguments are printed under the -*f* option).

> A process that has exited and has a parent, but has not yet been waited for by the parent (using the wait() system call), is marked <defunct>.

pwd – Print working directory name

The command *pwd* prints the path name of the working (current) directory to the standard output. The command is built into the Bourne shell *sh*.

---

pwd

If one of the error messages

```
Cannot open ...
```

or

```
Read error in ...
```

is printed, there is an error in the file system. Contact the system administrator.

Example

If you want to define your current directory to be your HOME directory.:

```
$ pwd
/usr/art/cobol/prg
$ HOME=`pwd`
$ echo $HOME
/usr/art/cobol/prg
```

rm – Remove files

rm removes the entries for one or more files from a directory. You can only remove entries if you have write permission for the parent directory.

---

rm[¬option]¬file...

If no option is given

> If you have write permissions for the *file*, *rm* will delete the entry without warning!
>
> If you do not have write permissions for *file* and the standard input is a terminal, the file's permissions will be printed followed by a question mark ?. This is a prompt for confirmation. If the answer begins with *y* (yes), the file is deleted, otherwise the file remains.

-f

> (f – force) The entries will be removed without prompting the user. In a write-protected directory, however, files are never removed.

-r

> You can specify a directory for *file*. *rm* will not print an error message as it would normally. *rm* recursively removes the contents of the directory and all the subdirectories. The directory will be emptied of files and itself removed.
>
> The parent directory (..) cannot be removed. With this option, symbolic links are not followed.
>
> If the removal of a non-empty, write-protected directory was attempted, the command will always fail (even if the *-f* option is used), resulting in an error message.

-i

> *rm* will interactively ask for confirmation of removal of every file or, if the option *-r* is used, for every directory.
>
> It overrides the *-f* option and remains in effect even if the standard input is not a terminal.

- -

> Use -- to mark the end of the options. This must be used if you need to give a file name that begins with -.

file

> Name of the file to be deleted. If the option *-r* is used, *file* can also be a directory. You can give one or more files or directories.
>
> If a file is given that has more than one link, the link itself is removed, not the file (the link count will be decremented by 1).

To be able to delete the file, you must have write permissions for the directory in which the file resides. However, to delete the file you do not need file read or write permissions.

Examples

Example 1
Remove all files that end with *.prog*, prompting for confirmation:

```
$ rm -i *.prog
ablauf.prog:? (y/n) y
code.prog:? (y/n) yuppers
eingabe.prog:? (y/n) n
zufall.prog:? (y/n) nope
a.prog:? (y/n) morgen
$
```

The links referencing *ablauf.prog* and *code.prog* are deleted; the others are not removed.

Example 2
Delete the directory *norm*, all the files contained in it, and all of its subdirectories.

```
$ rm -r norm
```

rmdir – Remove directories

rmdir removes one or more directories. *rmdir* cannot remove directories that still contain any objects. To remove a directory along with its underlying contents, you can use the command *rm* with the option *-r*.

---

rmdir [¬-p] [¬-s]¬directory¬...

No option given

> *rmdir* deletes the given directories.

-p

> (p – parents) The given directories will be removed as well as any parent directories that become empty when the given directory is removed. A message is printed to the standard output which indicates whether the complete path was removed or if part of the path remained.

-s

> (silent) The message from the *-p* option is suppressed.

directory

> Name of the directory to be deleted.

> You can give more than one directory name.

rsh – Execute a shell on a remote machine (remote shell)

---

rsh¬host[¬**-n**][¬**-l** login][¬command][¬option]

---

host

The name of the remote machine on which the shell should be executed.

The remote machine name must be entered in the file */etc/hosts* and/or in the database for Internet domain names. Every machine has an official name (the first entry in the database) and possibly one or more 'nicknames'. You can use any of the official names.

-n

This option is used when the standard output of the command should not be output on the remote machine. The standard output of *rsh* will be written to */dev/null*.

-l login

The account on the remote system with which the user wants to login. This is required if the account on the remote system has a different name from the user login on the local machine.

command

The UNIX command to be executed on the remote system.

If *command* is not given:

rsh uses *rlogin*, to log you into the remote system.

option

Arguments used by the command on the remote machine.

telnet – User interface for the TELNET protocol

telnet opens a session on a remote machine.

---

telnet [¬machine[¬port]]

---

machine
> is the name of the machine with which you want to connect. The connection to this machine will be established and *telnet* will be in input mode.
>
> If no machine name is given, *telnet* will work in command mode.

port
> is the port number of the port to be used.
>
> If no port number is given:
> The default port (TCP-23) will be used.

If the remote system is a UNIX system, the remote login will wait for the user login and the associated password. If both were entered correctly, *telnet* will enter input mode. You exit a *telnet* session with the command *close* or *quit. telnet* then returns to the command interpreter (shell).

TELNET commands

The following commands are available in command mode. You only need to enter as many of the first characters as are necessary to identify the command.

Initiate and end connection

open	open the connection to a remote machine
close	close all open connections
quit	close all open connections and end *telnet*

TELNET control

mode	toggle between character-by-character and line-by-line transmission
send	transfer special characters to the remote machine
set	change *telnet* variables or disable the associated function
toggle	toggle various functions
z	suspend *telnet*

Information about TELNET

?	help with *telnet* commands
status	list *telnet* status informationen
display	display some or all settings

uucp – UNIX to UNIX copy

uucp is used to send electronic mail to a remote machine and for copying files between UNIX systems.

---

uucp [¬option]...¬source-file¬...destination-file

-c

The source file will be copied to the *destination file*, and will not first copy the file into the spool directory. (This option is the default.)

-C

The source file will be copied into the spool directory for transfer later to *destination-file*.

-d

Create all necessary directories for the file copy. (This option is the default.)

-f

uucp should not create intermediate directories for the file copy.

-ggrade

This option sets the priority of the *uucp* file copy. *grade* is a single letter or digit: 0,...,9,A,...,Z,a,...,z. 0 indicates the highest priority, *z* the lowest. *uucp* sets the default priority to *Z*.

-j

Print the job identification number on the standard output.

-m

When the copy is complete, send mail to the user who made the *uucp* request.

-nuser_login

Notify the user on the remote system that a file was sent.

-r

Do not start the file transfer, just queue the job.

-sfile

Report status of the transfer to *file*. The option *-s* disables the *-m* option.

-x debug_level

Produce debugging information. The *debug_level* is a number between 0 and 9; higher numbers give more detailed information. This option is not necessarily implemented on all systems.

source-file

File that is to be copied.

destination-file

destination-file can be either a file or a directory. If you give a directory, the source files wil be copied into the directory under their simple file names.

Security

To ensure your system's security, file transfers using *uucp* should only take place using the public directory */var/spool/uucppublic*.

The number of files that are accessible from a remote machine can be limited, and they should be. You will probably not be allowed to retrieve files using the path name; instead, have the remote system user send you the files. For the same security reasons, you will not be allowed to send files to an arbitrary path name. The access permissions are controlled with the file */usr/lib/uucp/Permissions*.

All files received via *uucp* are owned by the UUCP administrator. *uucp* will not copy any files for which 'others' do not have read permission; in other words, the file must have at least the permissions 0444. During the file transfer *uucp* will change the file permissions to 0666.

who – Display the current system users

who lists information about system logins and logout.

who[¬option]...[¬file]	Format 1
who¬**-qn**¬number[¬file]	Format 2
who¬**am**¬**i**	Format 3
who¬**am**¬**I**	Format 4

Format 1: Output complete information

who[¬option]...[¬file]

If no option is given

> *who* lists the following information for each user currently logged in to the system:

- the login name of the user
- the name of the terminal where the user is logged in
- the time that the user logged in

-a

> (a – all) All options *-b, -d, -l, -p, -r, -t* and *-u* are enabled.

-b

> (b – boot) *who* will indicate the time and date of the last system reboot.

-d

> (d – dead) *who* will display all processes that have expired and not been respawned by *init*. If *-d* is activated with the option *-a*, the *exit* field will appear, containing the signal number that terminated the process. This can be useful in determining why a process terminated.

-H

> (H – headings) The option will print column headings above the regular output.

-l

> (l – login) This option lists only those terminals on which the system is waiting for someone to login. The *name* field is *LOGIN* in such cases. Other fields are the same as for user entries except that the *state* does not exist.

-p

> (p – process) *who* lists any processes that are currently active and have been previously spawned by init.

-q

> (q – quick) *who* displays only the names and the number of users currently logged on.

-r

> (r – run level) this option indicates the current run level of the *init*.

-s

> (s – standard) This option is the default and lists only the users currently logged in.

-T

> (T – Terminal) This option is the same as the *-s* option, except that the state of the terminal line is displayed. A plus + appears if the terminal is writable by anyone; a minus – appears if it is not. If this information cannot be determined, a question mark ? is printed.

-t

> (t – time) This option indicates the last change to the system clock (via the *date* command) by the system administrator.

-u

> (u – user) With this option *who* lists only those users who are currently logged in. The *idle* column gives information about the last input or output to the terminal: a dot (.) indicates that the terminal has seen activity in the last minute and is therefore 'current'. If more than 24 hours have elapsed or the line has not been used since boot time, the entry is marked *old*.

> The output field *PID* is the process-ID of the user's command interpreter (shell). The *comment* is the comment field associated with this terminal line as found in the file */etc/inittab*. For example, this can contain information about where the terminal is located.

file

> *who* examines this file, usually */var/adm/wtmp*, to obtain its information. *who* displays information about login activity and reboots of the system. The information can only go back to the last time the system administrator created or emptied *file*.

> If *file* is not given:

> *who* gets its information from the file */var/adm/utmp*.

Format 2: Output brief information

who¬-qn¬number[¬file]

-q

> see Format 1

-n¬number

> *who* prints *number* of users per line. *number* must be greater than 0.

file

> see Format 1

Format 3, Format 4: Display customized information

who¬am¬i
who¬am¬I
who prints:

- the user login in which you are currently logged in
- the name of the terminal (without */dev/*), on which you are logged in
- the initial login time.

write – Write to another user

With *write*, you can send messages to another user. *write* reads line by line from the standard input and sends the lines as messages to the user specified as recipient.

```
write¬recipient[¬tty-name]
text
...
...    END
```

---

recipient

> Login name of a user who is logged in on a terminal. You can also write to yourself. If a user is logged in on several terminals at once, you can specify the terminal.

> *who* can tell you the users currently logged in and their terminal numbers.

tty-name

> Number of the terminal where the recipient is logged in.

> If *tty-name* is not specified:

> *write* looks for the terminal in the file */var/adm/utmp*. If a user is logged on more than once, there will be several entries. *write* will use the first entry found and will print the following message:

```
user is logged on more than one place.
you are connected to "tyy-name".
Other locations are
tty-name
```

Security

A line that begins with the exclamation mark ! will be interpreted as a command; the remainder of the line will be passed on to the shell. The command will be executed and *write* remains active. Output that the command writes to the standard output is not included in the message.

6.2   System calls

Several of the system calls can become security problems, especially when return values are not checked and an error condition exists. Also, using system calls, you can check the security of a program. The references to other book pages for commands, system calls, and library routines refer to the *Programmer's Reference*. In addition, the references include the section number (in parentheses) of the *Programmer's Reference*. So, for example, the note 'see *fcntl*(2)' showing the section number (2) indicates that it is a system call. This is important to note since some names from manual pages differ only in the section number.

access – Ascertain access permissions on a file

```
#include <unistd.h>
int access(const char *path, int amode);
```

access checks the file given in *path* for accessibility according to the bit pattern contained in *amode*. *access* uses the real user ID in place of the effective user ID and the real group ID number in place of the effective group ID. The bit pattern in *amode* is constructed with a logical OR of the following constants (defined in *unistd.h*):

R_OK   test for read permission
W_OK   test for write permission
X_OK   test for execute (or search) permission
F_OK   check existence of the file

With *access* a program can check whether a user could gain access to the file without having the privileges granted by the program at the time of access. For example, a program could have to use files that are in a directory for which non-privileged users do not have read access. The programmer finds it acceptable to give the program set-UID and set-GID privileges, so that those files can be accessed. To insure that the user does not abuse the SUID and SGID privileges, the program will use *access* to check whether the user could access the file even without the SUID and GUID privileges. If the real user and group IDs used by *access* do not allow access, the program could refuse access.

Diagnostics

If the requested access is permitted, a value of 0 is returned. Otherwise, a value of -1 is returned and *errno* is set to indicate the error.

acct – *Enable or disable process accounting*

```
#include <unistd.h>
int acct(const char *path);
```

acct is used to enable or disable the system process accounting routine. If the routine is enabled, an accounting record will be written on an accounting file for each process that terminates. You can use accounting files to log the machine use of each user. Termination can be caused by one of two things: an *exit* call or a signal. The effective user ID of the calling process must be superuser to use this call.

path points to a pathname naming the accounting file.

The account routine is enabled if *path* is not (*char *)NULL* and no errors occur during the system call. It is disabled if *path* is null and no errors occur during the system call.

Diagnostics

Upon successful completion, a value of 0 is returned. Otherwise, a value of -1 is returned and *errno* is set to indicate the error.

chmod, fchmod – Change mode of file

```
#include <sys/types.h>
#include <sys/stat.h>
int chmod(const char *path, mode_t mode);
int fchmod(int fildes, mode_t mode);
```

chmod and *fchmod* set the access permission portion of the named file's mode according to the bit pattern contained in *mode*. The file is named either with *path*, which points to a path name, or by *fildes*, the file descriptor of the file. In order to be able to change the mode of a file, the effective user ID of the process must match the owner of the file or you must have the appropriate privileges.

If the process is not a privileged process and the file is not a directory, the mode bit 01000 (save text segment on execution) is cleared. If the process is not privileged and no member of the group list is privileged and the effective group ID of the process does not match the group ID of the file, then mode bit 02000 (set group ID on execution) is cleared.

If a 410 executable file has the sticky bit (mode bit 01000) set, the operating system will not delete the program text from the swap area when the last user process terminates. If a 413 or *ELF* executable file has the sticky bit set, the operating system will not delete the program text from memory when the last user process terminates.

If a directory is writable and the sticky bit is set, the files in the directory can only be deleted or renamed if one of the following conditions are met:

> the file belongs to the user
> the directory belongs to the user
> the user has write permissions for the file
> the user is a privileged user.

If the mode bit 02000 is set (set group ID on execution) and the mode bit 00010 is not set (search and execute by group) mandatory file/record locking will exist on a regular file.

Diagnostics

Upon successful completion, a value of 0 is returned. Otherwise, a value of -1 is returned and *errno* is set to indicate the error.

chroot – Change root directory

```
#include <unistd.h>
int chroot(const char *path);
```

path points to a path name naming a directory. *chroot* causes the named directory to become the root directory, the starting point for path searches for path names beginning with /. The user's current working directory is unaffected by the *chroot* system call. To be able to change the root directory, the effective user ID of the process must be that of the system administrator.

The '. .' entry in the root directory is interpreted to mean the root directory itself. Thus, '. .' cannot be used to access files outside the subtree rooted at the root directory.

Diagnostics

Upon successful completion, a value of 0 is returned. Otherwise, a value of -1 is returned and *errno* is set to indicate the error.

exec – Execute a file

```
#include <unistd.h>
int execl (const char *path, const char *arg0,
..., const char *argn, (char *)0);
int execv (const char *path, char *const *argv);
int execle (const char *path, const char *arg0,
..., const char *argn, (char *0), const char
*envp[ ]);
int execve (const char *path, const char *argv,
const char *envp[ ]);
int execlp (const char *File, const char *arg0,
..., const char *argn, (char *)0);
int execvp (const char *File, char *const
*argv);
```

exec in all its forms transforms the calling process into a new process. The new process is constructed from an ordinary, executable file. This file is either an executable object file or a data file for an interpreter. There can be no return from a successful *exec* call because the calling process is overlaid by the new process.

path points to a path name that identifies the new process file.

File points to the new process file. If the string *File* includes a slash, then this argument represents the path name of the file. Otherwise, the path prefix for this file is obtained by a search of the directories passed as the environment variable *PATH*. The environment is typically supplied by the shell.

File descriptors open in the calling process remain open in the new process, except for those whose close-on-exec flag is set (see *fcntl(2)*). For those file descriptors that remain open, the file pointer is unchanged. Therefore, before an *exec* function call, programs should close all files that are no longer needed.

Diagnostics

If *exec* returns to the calling process, a value of -1 is returned and *errno* is set to indicate the error.

exit, _exit – Terminate a process

```
#include <stdlib.h>
void exit(int status);
#include <unistd.h>
void _exit(int status);
```

The *exit* function calls all the functions that were entered with the command *at-exit*, in reverse entry order (last in first out). The function *_exit* circumvents the processing of these functions.

If a function entered with *atexit()* does not return a value, then the remaining functions will not be called and the *exit* process stops.

If *exit* is called more than once, its behaviour is undefined.

After all the entered functions have been processed, *exit* flushes all output streams, closes all open data streams and removes all files created using *tmpfile()*.

exit and *_exit* terminate the calling process as follows:

- All of the open files, directories, and message catalogue descriptors of the calling process are closed.

- The signal *SIGCHLD* (death of child) is set to the parent process.

- If the parent process of the calling process did not set the option *SA_NOCLDWAIT*, then the calling process is transformed into a zombie process. A zombie process only occupies a slot in the process table. It has no other space allocated either in user or kernel space. The process table slot that it occupies is partially overlaid with time accounting information to be used by *times*.

- The parent process ID of all of the calling processes' existing child processes and zombie processes is set to 1. This means the initialization process inherits each of these processes.

- Each attached shared memory segment is detached and the value of *shm_nattach* in the data structure associated with its shared memory identifier is decremented by 1.

- For each semaphore for which the calling process has set a *semadj* value, that *semadj* value is added to the *semval* of the specified semaphore.

- If the process has a process, text, or data lock, an UNLOCK is performed.

- An accounting record is written on the accounting file if the system's accounting routine is enabled (see *acct(2)*).

- If the process is a controlling process *SIGHUP* will be sent to the process group in the foreground of its controlling terminal and the terminal will be made available.

- If the calling process has any children whose process group will be orphaned when the calling process terminates, or if the calling process is an element of a process group that will be orphaned when the calling process ends, then the signals *SIGHUP* and *SIGCONT* will be sent to this process group.

The symbolic constants *EXIT_SUCCESS* and *EXIT_FAILURE* are defined in *stdlib.h* and can be used for comparing the *status* value to check for success or failure.

fork – Create a new process

```
#include <sys/types.h>
#include <unistd.h>
pid_t fork(void);
```

---

fork causes the creation of a new process. The new process (child process) is an exact copy of the calling process (parent process).

Upon successful completion, *fork* returns a value of 0 to the child process and returns the process ID of the child process to the parent process. Otherwise, a value of (*pid_t*) - 1 is returned to the parent process, no child process is created, and *errno* is set to indicate the error. *fork* can fail if the amount of memory available is insufficient to create a new process or if the process table limit would be exceeded if the new process were created.

The child process differs from the parent process in the following ways:

- Process locks, text locks and data locks are not inherited by the child.

- The child process has a unique process ID, which differs from all other process group IDs.

- The child process has a different parent process ID (that is, the process ID of the parent process).

- The child process has its own copy of the parent's file descriptors and directory stream. Each of the child's file descriptors shares a common file pointer with the corresponding file descriptor of the parent.

- All *semadj* values are cleared.

- The *tms* structure of the child process is as follows: *tms_utime*, *stime*, *cutime*, and *cstime* are set to 0.

- The time left until an alarm clock signal is reset to 0.

- The set of signals that are to be exported to the process is initialized to the empty set.

kill – Send a signal to a process or a group of processes

```
#include <sys/types.h>
#include <signal.h>
int kill(pid_t pid, int sig);
```

kill sends a signal to a process or a group of processes. The process or group of processes to which the signal is to be sent is specified by *pid*. The signal that is to be sent is specified by *sig* and is either one from the list given in *signal*, or 0. If *sig* is 0 (the null signal), error checking is performed but no signal is actually sent. This can be used to check the validity of *pid*.

Because *_POSIX_SAVED_IDS* is set by the system, the real or effective UID of the sending process must match the secured (by *exec*(2)) UID of the receiving process if the effective UID of the sender is not the system administrator, or if *sig* is *SIGCONT* and the sender has the same session ID as the receiver.

The processes with a process ID of 0 and a process ID of 1 are special system processes and will be referred to below as *proc0* and *proc1*, respectively.

If *pid* is greater than zero, *sig* will be sent to the process whose process ID is equal to *pid*. *pid* may equal 1. If *pid* is negative but (*pid_t*) is not -1, *sig* will be sent to all processes whose process group ID is equal to the absolute value of *pid* and for which the process has permission to send a signal. If *pid* (*pid_t*) is 0, *sig* will be sent to all processes excluding *proc0* and *proc1* whose process group ID is equal to the process group ID of the sender. Permission is necessary to send a signal. If *pid* (*pid_t*) is -1 and the effective user ID of the sender is not the system administrator, *sig* will be sent to all processes excluding *proc0* and *proc1* whose real user ID is equal to the effective user ID of the sender. If *pid* (*pid_t*) is -1 and the effective user ID of the sender is the system administrator, *sig* will be sent to all processes excluding *proc0* and *proc1*.

Diagnostics

Upon successful completion, a value of 0 is returned. Otherwise, a value of -1 is returned and errno is set to indicate the error.

open – Open a file for reading or writing

```
#include <sys/types.h>
#include <sys/stat.h>
#include <fcntl.h>
int open (const char *path, int oflag, ...
/* mode_t mode */);
```

path points to a path name naming a file. *open* opens a file descriptor for the named file and sets the file status flags according to the value of *oflag*.

If the *O_CREAT* bit of *oflag* is set and the file does not yet exist, after completing successfully *open* will update the file's *st_atime*, *st_ctime*, and *st_mtime* fields and the fields *st_ctime* and *st_mtime* of the parent directory. An *open* with *O_CREAT* set will not be successful unless the calling process has read and write permissions for the directory in which the file is to be created. The access permissions of the new file comprise the third argument to *open* and can be changed with the user's *umask* setting. If *open* is called to open a file, without having *O_CREAT* set, and that file does not yet exist, *open* will fail.

If the *O_TRUNC* bit is set and the file already exists, *open* will update the fields *st_ctime* and *st_mtime* upon successful completion.

Diagnostics

Upon successful completion, the file descriptor is returned. Otherwise, a value of -1 is returned and *errno* is set to indicate the error.

read, readv – Read from a file

```
#include <sys/types.h>
#include <sys/uio.h>
#include <unistd.h>
ssize_t read(int fildes, void *buf, size_t
nbyte);
int readv(int fildes, struct iovec *iov, int
iovcnt);
```

read attempts to read *nbyte* bytes from the file associated with *fildes* into the buffer pointed to by *buf*. If *nbyte* is null, *read* will return null and will have no other effect. *fildes* is a file descriptor that has been returned from one of the system calls *creat, open, dup, fcntl,* or *pipe. read* is not concerned with the access permissions of the file. As soon as a file is opened for read, *read* will be able to get information from the file, even if the permissions for the file were changed after it was opened.

When attempting to read from a regular file with file locking set (see *chmod(2))* , and there is a blocking (that is, owned by another process) write lock on the segment of the file to be read:

- If *O_NONBLOCK* is set, *read* will return a -1 and set *errno* to *EAGAIN.*
- If *O_NONBLOCK* is not set, *read* will sleep until the blocking record lock is removed.

Attempting to read from an empty pipe (or FIFO) will have the following effects:

- If no other process has the file open for write, *read* will return the value 0 indicating the end of the file.
- If a process has the file open for write and *O_NONBLOCK* is set, *read* will return -1 and set *errno* to *EAGAIN.*
- If *O_NONBLOCK* is clear, *read* will block until data is written to the pipe or until the pipe is closed by all processes that had it open for write.

When attempting to read a file associated with a terminal that has no data currently available:

- If *O_NONBLOCK* is set, *read* will return a -1 and set *errno* to *EAGAIN.*
- If *O_NONBLOCK* is clear, *read* will block until data becomes available.

When attempting to read a file associated with a stream that is neither a pipe nor a terminal file and that has no data currently available:

- If *O_NONBLOCK* is set, *read* will return -1 and set *errno* to *EAGAIN*.

- If *O_NONBLOCK* is clear, *read* will block until data becomes available.

When reading from a STREAMS file, handling of zero-byte messages is determined by the current read mode setting. In *byte-stream* mode, *read* accepts data until it has read *nbyte* bytes, or until there is no more data to read, or until a zero-byte message block is encountered. *read* then returns the number of bytes read. It then places the zero-byte message back on the stream to be retrieved by the next *read* or *getmsg* (see *getmsg(2)*). In the two other modes, a zero-byte message returns a value of 0 and the message is removed from the stream. When a zero-byte message is read as the first message on a stream, a value of 0 is returned regardless of the read mode.

Ordinarily, a *read* from a STREAMS file can only process data messages. *read* cannot process any type of control message and will fail if a control message is encountered at the stream head. This default behaviour can be altered by using *I_SRDOPT ioctl(2)* to replace the stream into a control-data mode or into a mode in which all protocol information is removed. In control-data mode, control messages are discarded by *read*, but any data associated with the control messages is returned to user.

Diagnostics

Upon successful completion a non-negative integer is returned indicating the number of bytes actually read. Otherwise, -1 is returned and *errno* is set to indicate the error.

write, writev – Write on a file

```
#include <unistd.h>
ssize_t write(int fildes, const void *buf,
size_t nbyte);
#include <sys/types.h>
#include <sys/uio.h>
int writev(int fildes, const struct iovec *iov,
int iovcnt);
```

write attempts to write *nbyte* bytes from the buffer pointed to by *buf* to the file asso-ciated with the file descriptor *fildes*. If *nbyte* is null and the file is a regular file, *write* will return null and will have no other effect. *fildes* is a file descriptor that has been returned from one of the system calls *creat, open, dup, fcntl,* or *pipe*.

writev does the same as *write*, except that it collects the output data of the *iovcnt* buffers that are defined by the members of the *iov* fields (*iov*[0], *iov*[1], ..., *iov*[*iovcnt* - 1]). *iovcnt* is valid if it is greater than 0 and less than or equal to *IOV_MAX*.

A *write* to a regular file will be blocked if file locking is set (see *chmod(2)*), and there is a record lock owned by another process on the segment of the file to be written.

- If *O_NDELAY* or *O_NONBLOCK* is set, *write* will return a -1 and set *errno* to *EAGAIN*.

- If neither *O_NDELAY* nor *O_NONBLOCK* is set, *write* will sleep until all blocking record locks are removed, or until *write* is terminated with a signal.

If a *write* requests that more bytes be written than there is room for – for exam-ple the upper limit for process file sizes, the upper limit for system file sizes or the physical end of a medium – only as many bytes as there is room for will be written. For example, suppose there is space for 20 bytes more in a file before reaching a limit. A *write* of 512 bytes will return 20. The next *write* of a non-zero number of bytes will give a failure return (except with pipes and FIFO files).

Write requests to a pipe or FIFO file are handled in the same way as those to regular files, with the following exceptions:

- There is no file positioning with pipes, and consequently every write request is written to the end of the pipe. Write requests of *PIPE_BUF* or fewer bytes will not overlap on data of other processes that are writing to the same pipe. Write tasks that are larger than *PIPE_BUF* bytes can over-lap the arbitrary bounds of other processes' write tasks, regardless of whether the *O_NONBLOCK* or *O_NDELAY* option is set.

- If *O_NONBLOCK* and *O_NDELAY* are not set, a write task can block a process; however, typically a value of *nbyte* is returned.

- If *O_NONBLOCK* is set, *write* requests will be handled as follows: write requests for *PIPE_BUF* or fewer bytes are either successfully executed and return *nbyte*, or they return a value of -1 and set *errno* to *EAGAIN*. A *write* request for more than *PIPE_BUF* bytes transfers either as many as it can and returns the number of bytes written, or it doesn't transfer any data and returns a value of -1 and sets *errno* to *EAGAIN*. Even if a request is for more than *PIPE_BUF* bytes and all data written to the pipe has already been read, *write* will still transfer at least *PIPE_BUF* bytes.

- If *O_NDELAY* is set, *write* requests will be handled as follows: *write* will not block the process; write requests for *PIPE_BUF* or fewer bytes are either executed in their entirety, returning *nbyte*, or they return a value of 0. A *write* request for more than *PIPE_BUF* bytes transfers either as many as it can and returns the number of bytes written, or it doesn't transfer any data and returns a value of 0. If a request is for more than *PIPE_BUF* bytes and all data written to the pipe has already been read, *write* will still transfer at least *PIPE_BUF* bytes.

When attempting to write to a file descriptor (not a pipe or FIFO file) that supports writes without blocking and that cannot accept the data immediately:

- If *O_NONBLOCK* and *O_NDELAY* are not set, *write* will block until the data can be accepted.

- If either *O_NONBLOCK* or *O_NDELAY* is set, *write* will not block the process. If some of the data can be written without blocking the process, it will write as much as possible and return the value of the number of bytes written. Otherwise, if *O_NONBLOCK* is set it will return a value of -1 and set *errno* to *EAGAIN* or, if *O_NDELAY* is set, it will return 0.

For STREAMS files, the operation of *write* is determined by the values of the minimum and maximum *nbyte* range ('packet size') accepted by the stream. These values are contained in the topmost stream module. Unless the user pushes the topmost module, these values cannot be set or tested from user level. If *nbyte* falls within the packet size range, *nbyte* bytes will be written.

If *nbyte* does not fall within the range and the minimum packet size value is zero, *write* will break the buffer into maximum packet size segments prior to sending the data downstream (the last segment may contain less than the maximum packet size). If *nbyte* does not fall within the range and the minimum value is non-zero, *write* will fail with *errno* set to *ERANGE*. Writing a zero-length buffer (*nbyte* is zero) to a STREAMS device sends a zero byte message with zero returned. However, if a zero-length buffer is written to a pipe or FIFO file, nothing is sent and no value is returned. To be able to send empty messages through a pipe or FIFO file, the user program can use *I_SWROPT ioctl*(2).

Writing to a stream causes messages that have a priority class of zero to be created. When writing to a stream that is not a pipe or FIFO file, the following are true:

- If *O_NDELAY* and *O_NONBLOCK* are not set and the stream cannot accept data (the stream write queue is full owing to internal flow control conditions), *write* will block until data can be accepted.

- If *O_NDELAY* or *O_NONBLOCK* is set and the stream cannot accept any data, *write* will return a value of -1 and set *errno* to *EAGAIN*.

- If either *O_NDELAY* or *O_NONBLOCK* is set and part of the buffer is already written when a condition in which the stream cannot accept additional data occurs, *write* will terminate and return the number of bytes successfully written.

Diagnostics

Upon successful completion, the number of bytes actually written is returned. Otherwise, a value of -1 is returned and *errno* is set to indicate the error.

Index